D0846165

597
FER

Ferraris, Carl, Jr. (Dr)
Catfish in the aquarium.

DATE DUE

APR 1 3 2002			
APR 1 3 2002			
ILL 18			

Catfish
in the Aquarium

An Introduction to Catfish Keeping
and the Diversity of Catfish Forms and Behavior

by
Dr. Carl Ferraris, Jr.

⊙ Tetra

Tetra Press
CATFISH IN THE AQUARIUM
A Tetra Press Publication
By Dr. Carl Ferraris, Jr.

Copyright © 1991 Tetra Sales USA
A Division of Warner Lambert
201 Tabor Rd.
Morris Plains, N.J. 07950
All rights reserved

ISBN: 3-89356-043-2
Library of Congress Catalog Card Number: 90-70157
Tetra Press Item Number: 16015
Production services by Martin Cook Associates, Ltd., New York

Printed in Hong Kong

First edition
10 9 8 7 6 5 4 3 2 1

Contents

HANOVER TOWNSHIP LIBRARY
P.O. BOX 475
HANOVER, IL. 61041-0475

Preface

Of the many beautiful and interesting species of fish available to tropical fish keepers, none are more universal and desirable than catfish. Almost every aquarium has a place for these fascinating, diligent creatures. Their unique shapes, varying sizes and colors, and excellent work habits make them both a visually interesting part of and contributing members to millions of aquariums.

Tetra Press is particularly pleased to publish *Catfish in the Aquarium,* which reviews with photographs and relevant detail the important members of this group. We are both pleased and privileged to have Dr. Carl Ferraris, Jr., author this work. His years of study, both in local habitat and as an aquarist, immensely qualify him as one of the world's true authorities on catfish.

—Tetra Press

Acknowledgments

Paul Loiselle first suggested that I write this book. Ginny Eckstein generously shared with me her observations and ideas about catfishes and her fish room so that I could see for myself much of what she first observed. John O'Malley, Mark Smith, and Paul Loiselle allowed me to retain their outstanding collections of catfish photographs, from which most of the illustrations in this book come. Bob Padron always welcomed me into his fish room, even at the busiest of times, so that I could observe the unusual catfishes that he would go out of his way to find for me. Ginny Eckstein, Mario de Pinna, Susana Ferraris, and, most especially, Helena Andreyco read parts of this book and provided many useful comments. Alexia Dorszynski provided much useful information on writing and editing. Last, but not least, Alan Mintz provided needed encouragement and technical support throughout the overlong period during which the book was being written. Without the help of all of these people, this book might never have been finished; my thanks go to them.

Glossary

Adipose fin (or adipose dorsal fin): A structure on the posterior half of the dorsal surface (back) of nearly all catfishes. It may appear as a tab of skin or a long, low ridge that extends from behind the dorsal fin to the caudal fin. Unlike the other fins in catfishes, the adipose fin usually does not have any rays or other bony supports.

Barbels: Threadlike projections that extend from the corners of the mouth or beneath the chin of catfishes. Often called "whiskers," barbels are covered with taste buds.

Benthic: Referring to something associated with the bottom of a lake, river, or ocean. A benthic catfish is found near the bottom and not in midwater.

Blackwater: Water containing high concentrations of dissolved tannins and little or no silt. It is usually found in rivers that run through thick tropical forests. Because of the tannins, blackwaters are usually acidic, sometimes reaching a pH of 4 or less.

Brackish water: Water that contains some amount of salt, but not as high a concentration as found in seawater. Brackish water is usually found along the margins of islands and continents, especially near the mouths of rivers.

Buccal cavity: The region inside the mouth.

Cleithral bone: One of the main support bones for the pectoral fin. In catfishes the cleithral bone (or cleithrum) often has a posteriorly projecting spine just above the base of the pectoral fin.

Congener: One of two or more species belonging to the same genus.

Conspecific: Belonging to the same species.

Contaminant: A fish not belonging to the same species as the majority of the fishes in a shipment. This term is used by fish importers and wholesalers when referring to an unexpected fish found among more common aquarium species.

Dimorphic: Having two forms. Often, male and female catfish of the same species are quite distinct in appearance due to differences in structure or coloration. Such species are said to be sexually dimorphic.

Dorsal fin: A fin on the dorsal surface (back) of the fish. Usually the fin is found just behind the head, although it may be located in the middle of the back. In many catfishes the dorsal fin has a large, hardened ray, called the dorsal fin spine, at the beginning of the fin.

Estuarine: Associated with an estuary.

Fry: A young fish.

Mental barbels: Barbels on the chin.

Monotypic: Referring to a genus or family that contains only a single species.

Nocturnal: Active at night.

Nuchal shield: A bony plate between the back of the head and the dorsal fin.

Oddball: A specimen of any species that is not frequently seen in the aquarium hobby.

Odontodes: Bristlelike structures on the surface of certain catfishes, especially members of the families Callichthyidae and Loricariidae.

Odontodes may be found scattered over the body or concentrated in patches on or near the head.

Operculum: A bony flap, located just behind the head on each side of the body, that protects the gills. Often called an opercle.

Oral brooding: Retention of developing eggs and fry in the mouth of one of the parents. Also called oral incubation.

Rays (or fin rays): Bony, rodlike elements, often branched, that together with a fine, flexible membrane make up the fins in all bony fishes.

Rictal barbels: Barbels that project from the corners of the mouth.

Scutes: Bony plates on the surface of the skin. Unlike scales, scutes cannot be removed easily from the skin.

Serrae: A row of small spines or recurved points, similar to the cutting edge of a steak knife, along the dorsal or pectoral spine or the cleithrum.

Sp.: Abbreviation of *species* (singular). It is used only after a genus name, usually to indicate that it was not possible to identify the species of a particular fish. For example: Long, slender barbels are evident in the juvenile tiger shovel nose (*Pseudoplatystoma* sp.).

Speciose: Usually referring to a genus or family that has a large number of species.

Spines: Thick, inflexible rays. In many catfishes the first ray of the pectoral fin and the first long ray of the dorsal fin are in the form of spines.

Spp.: Abbreviation of *species* (plural). It is used only after a genus name, when referring to more than one species. For example: *Corydoras* spp. are desirable aquarium residents.

Substratum: The material, such as rocks, gravel, and sunken wood, that makes up the bottom of rivers, lakes, or aquaria.

The catfish *Synodontis ornatipinnis*. Photo by: M. Smith.

What Is a Catfish?

Who's Who?

The late Dr. Archie Carr of the University of Florida once wrote, "Any damn fool knows a catfish!" Although he was referring at the time only to North American catfishes, the statement can equally be true of catfishes worldwide. Catfishes are so distinctive in appearance that there is little need to provide a formal definition for anyone who has ever seen them. A mouth surrounded by "whiskers," a thick-skinned, scaleless body, and a trio of formidable spines surrounding a broad, flattened head are usually sufficient to identify a typical catfish.

Although not all catfishes look exactly like that, these features are an important part of the scientific definition of these fishes. The "whiskers," for example, are known as barbels, and at least one pair can be found on every catfish. Scales, similar in appearance to those found on trout or carp, are never found on catfishes, whose skin is either naked or covered to some extent with nonremovable bony plates, or armor.

In addition to these characteristics, scientists have discovered a whole host of features of catfish anatomy that are unique to them. This suggests that all living catfishes probably de-

Chrysichthys walkeri. Photo by: P. Loiselle.

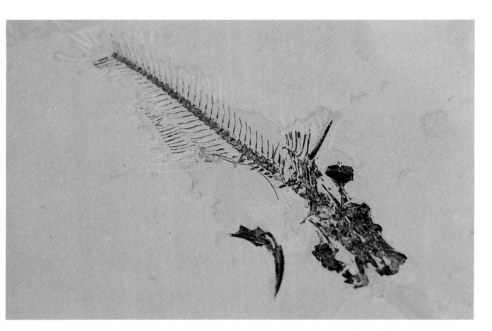

An unnamed fossilized catfish from Argentina. *Photo by:* C. Ferraris.

scended from a single ancestral catfish species that lived during the height of the dinosaur era.

Most catfishes are readily recognized as such even by beginning hobbyists. Sometimes the heavily protected, mail-coated bodies of species of the families Loricariidae and Callichthyidae make it difficult to believe that they can be closely related to the more typically shaped pimelodids or bagrids, but on close examination almost everyone quickly picks up the similarities between these groups. About the only time people seem to be fooled is when they encounter catfishes that lack barbels—or at least seem to. Several species of free-swimming catfishes have very tiny barbels, or the barbels are hidden in grooves in the cheek. When these fishes are actively moving about, the barbels can be overlooked easily, leaving in doubt the identity of the fish.

A close look is usually sufficient, however, to tell that an iridescent shark (genus *Pangasius*) or species of the genus *Ageneiosus* is really a catfish. Too, a few catfishes have very elongated, slender bodies that look anything but catfish-like. Several species of the walking catfish family Clariidae and numerous pencil-thin species of parasitic catfishes, family Trichomycteridae, are among the least catfish-looking catfishes, appearing more similar to eels.

In contrast, only a very few noncatfishes can be mistaken for a catfish. Some loaches have mouths that are surrounded with barbels, but a close look reveals that the barbels are often arranged on the upper lip of the loach's mouth—something that is never seen in catfishes. Loaches also

9

Fossilized remains of a mass mortality of *Corydoras* from Argentina, probably due to the fish being trapped in a pond that dried out before the onset of the rainy season. *Photo by:* C. Ferraris.

A loach of the genus *Botia.* *Photo by:* P. Loiselle.

Labeo bicolor, the red-tailed shark.
Photo by: Tetra Archives.

have scales on their body (even if very small scales sometimes), which also readily distinguishes them from the scaleless catfishes. Some members of the minnow family that are called "sharks" (for example, the black shark or the red-tail black shark) also have been called catfish, presumably because of their barbels, but their obvious body scales are enough to eliminate them from being considered catfish.

The name "catfish" goes at least as far back as 1816, when Georges Cuvier used the term *poisson-chat* (fish-cat) in reference to the North American white catfish, *Ictalurus catus.* Since then the name has become synonymous with the entire group of more than 2500 species.

Catfishes are found on all continents except Antarctica, and are sometimes dominant in the waters in which they are found. Their variation in form and behavior is staggering. In a single river system in South America or southern Asia, where catfishes are particularly abundant, it is possible to find catfishes active day and night: some species grazing off algae-covered rocks or logs, others picking minute animal life out of their hiding places, and still others actively preying on fishes, including different species of catfish. Recent evidence suggests that, like termites, at least some species of the armored Loricariidae family

11

can even digest wood, with the help of microbes that reside permanently in the catfish's gut.

Not only are catfishes found throughout the continents, they inhabit diverse habitats within continents. Some species can be found in estuaries and occasionally even in true seawater throughout much of the northern part of South America. Closely related species that require the softest of waters exist only in tropical rain forests, and any amount of dissolved salts seems to be sufficient to stress their physiology. While catfishes are found in lowland rivers, at or just above sea level, they have also

World distribution of catfishes (see shaded areas). *Illustration by:* Aquarium Digest International Archives.

been found at some of the highest elevations recorded for freshwater fishes in the Himalayas and the South American Andes (more than 14,000 feet above sea level). There are very few freshwater environments that are not home to some species of catfish. In fact, some catfishes are at home in coral reefs. A few species of the Australia–New Guinean family Plotosidae have exploited the marine environment and become lifelong residents of reefs and near-shore areas from South Africa to Japan.

Catfish range in size from among the smallest known freshwater fishes to the largest. More than two dozen species of South American catfishes never grow to more than 1 inch in length, and some of those species remain pencil-thin. One of the smallest,

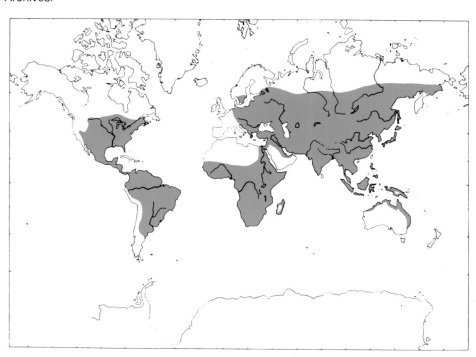

Pangasianodon gigas, one of the world's largest catfishes, from the Mekong River. Photo by: H. M. Smith.

Scoloplax dicra, barely reaches more than ½ inch at maturity. In contrast, a list of the largest species known from the freshwaters of each continent would include at least one catfish, and in some places catfish dominate such lists. For example, although there are only two species of catfish native to Europe, one, the wels (Silurus glanis), was reported to grow to more than 16 feet in length and weigh in excess of 650 pounds, making it one of the largest known species of freshwater fishes anywhere. The main river systems of Southeast Asia host at least two species of extraordinarily large pangasiid catfishes, Pangasianodon gigas and the long-finned iridescent shark, Pangasius sanitwongsei. Each of these species has been reported to grow in excess of 9 feet in length. In South America a number of species of pimelodid catfishes routinely reach lengths of more than 4 feet and weigh more than 100 pounds, leaving only the pirarucu (Arapaima gigas) as a larger fish. Even the rela-

tively small North American ictalurids include the blue cat, Ictalurus furcatus, and the flathead catfish, Pylodictus olivaris, which exceed 5 feet in length and reach nearly 100 pounds. The African freshwater rivers are home to species of the bagrid Chrysichthys, reportedly one of the largest known fishes in those waters.

Unfortunately, all of these reports of large fishes are accompanied by statements that the giants are much rarer now than formerly, according to local fishermen. Even in the Amazon River system, the large catfishes are being removed at such a rate that the normal population level cannot be sustained. Because of this trend, without careful management large catfishes, like most other giant freshwater fishes, will become a thing of the past. Fortunately, management is now beginning, and in Southeast Asia the two

13

Sorubimichthys planiceps, a full-sized shovel nose catfish. *Photo by:* C. Ferraris.

giant pangasiids are protected species, which cannot be exported until local efforts to stabilize the population have succeeded. For aquarists, this means the loss to the hobby, at least temporarily, of the most attractive species of this family. But if conservation efforts succeed, young specimens of the long-finned iridescent shark may once again be available.

Scientific Names

It is often said that having to learn the scientific names of fishes is among the most intimidating aspects of the aquarium hobby. Often both family and species names are long and unfamiliar, and learning them may seem unnecessarily burdensome. For many species, however, scientific names are the only names these fish have. This is especially true of rare species that have only recently become incorporated into the aquarium hobby. In time many of them will acquire a common name in the English language that can, for all intents and purposes, replace the scientific name in much of the hobbyist literature—*if* everybody agrees to use the same name. This kind of standardization of English names does not exist now and is one of several worthy projects that could be undertaken by a society of catfish hobbyists (more on such groups in the chapter "Beyond This Book").

Even after common names replace scientific names in the hobby, it will still be important to learn the scientific names and understand their use. The scientific literature will still be written almost exclusively using these names, and the hobbyist's ability to find additional information on a species will depend on knowing them. With so little information on the biology of catfishes currently available to hobbyists, someone wishing to learn more about a particular catfish may have to dig into the more technical literature (see "Beyond This Book" for information on how to begin a search through the scientific literature). Because of this, I am providing a brief summary of the formation and use of scientific names.

Every time a new species of catfish (or any animal or plant, for that matter) is discovered, it is introduced in the scientific literature with a two-part name, a system devised by Linnaeus in the mid-1700s and the generally accepted standard ever since. The first part, the genus name, is used to indicate the similarity of one species to others. The genus name, which always begins with a capital letter, may be used by itself when discussing all of the species belonging to that genus. The second part is the specific name (not the species name, which refers only to the combined genus and specific names). In contrast to the genus name, the specific name is never capitalized and is never used alone in properly written literature. This rule prevents confusion, because more than one species can have the same specific name, but only one species can have the genus and specific names in combination. For example, it may be perfectly clear to you that "brichardi" refers to the exquisite African catfish *Synodontis brichardi,* but someone else may think you mean *Tropheus brichardi, Lamprologus brichardi, Teleogramma brichardi,* or any of several other species of African freshwater fishes named in honor of Pierre Brichard.

The rules that govern correct scientific naming are quite complex and getting more so every year. In general, one of the most important rules states that the correct specific name is the one first proposed for a species; any name proposed after the first must give way to the earlier name unless a good reason exists for not using the older name. One problem with this rule is that scientists are still discovering older names for fishes and therefore changing the scientific names of fishes to conform with this rule. These changes can be irritating to hobbyists and scientists alike, but no workable alternative has yet been proposed that would not cause even more confusion.

However, the frequency of these name changes seems to be decreasing. More often it is the genus name

and not the specific name that changes. This leaves readers feeling unsettled—they *think* they know which fish is being discussed, but are not quite sure.

The genus name serves two functions. It is a necessary part of the species name, but it is also used as an indication of similarity. The problem is that people have different ideas of how similar two species need be in order to be included in the same genus. There is also disagreement about what is meant by similarity. Some people interpret it to mean genealogical similarity—that is, similarity derived from an evolutionary perspective—while others believe it relates to the overall appearance of species. These two views (and there are a number of others) cause a great deal of disagreement about what species should be joined together into genera, and even into families. For example, the well-known armored catfishes that we all now refer to as members of the genus *Corydoras* are quite diverse in their form and biology. As we learn more about the nearly 100 species that are currently recognized, it is likely that someone will suggest that a species be broken up into two or more genera. Some species that we now call *Corydoras* may be known by another genus name by the next generation of aquarists.

The conventions governing the pronunciation of family names are comparatively straightforward. It should be noted that the guide I present here is based on American English pronunciation. While scientific names are a universal standard for written communication, pronunciation is so heavily influenced by cultural linguistic overtones that it may not be possible to standardize the pronunciation of

15

scientific names. Thus, this guide will be most useful to Americans talking among themselves and to non-Americans who need to understand names as Americans pronounce them.

All family names end with the letters *-idae*. This is pronounced in a number of ways, including "ah day," "id dee," and crosses between these two: "id day" and "ah dee." I use "id dee" and therefore have written it this way in the pronunciation guide for each family. The root of the family name comes from one genus (called the type genus) included in the family—for example, Doradidae from *Doras,* Auchenipteridae from *Auchenipterus,* and Ariidae from *Arius.* In pronouncing the family name, the emphasis, or stress, is placed on the last syllable of the root, or just before the *-idae* ending. In the pronunciation guide, the stressed syllable is capitalized. Using the examples mentioned previously, the family names should be pronounced "dor ADD id dee," "ow can ip TARE id dee," and "air REE id dee." Family names are often shortened in both conversation and informal written articles (as they are in this book). Instead of including the entire suffix *-idae,* only *-id* is used. So members of the Callichthyidae are referred to as "callichthyids," and a trait of this family is a callichthyid characteristic. Note that the informal use of a family name does not begin with a capital letter, unlike the formal name, which always does.

Pronunciation of species names is a little more difficult to summarize, in part due to the vast number of names and their variations. Usually, the next to the last syllable is stressed in names of genera. Thus, the name for the African upside-down catfishes, *Synodontis,* is pronounced "sin oh DON tis," and the rare South American tiger-striped catfish *Merodontotus* is pronounced "meer oh don TOE dus" (and definitely not "meer oh DON tus," which I often hear!). There are a few exceptions to this rule, and one of the most widespread relates to names ending in *-ia* or *-ius.* When this is seen, it is the third to the last, or antepenultimate, syllable that receives the stress. So *Peckoltia* is pronounced "peh KOLE tee ah" and not "peh kole TEE ah," and *Loricaria* is pronounced "lore ah KARE ee ah" and not "lore ah kare EE ah."

Specific names are pronounced with the stress usually on the second to the last syllable. However, names ending with *-i* or *-ii,* which are almost always preceded by the family name of a man for whom the species is named (called a patronym), are usually given the typical pronunciation of the name followed by either "ee" (pronounced "ē") or "ie" (pronounced "ī") or, if spelled with a double *i,* "ee ie." Thus, *Amblydoras hancocki* would be pronounced "am blee DORE us HAN cock ie," and *Brochis britskii* is "BROH kiss BRIT skee ie." Species named to honor women end in *-ae* (pronounced to rhyme with "pay"). Very few catfishes have been named for women, but one popular aquarium resident so named is *Corydoras robineae.*

Catfish Anatomy

The chapter "Catfishes of the World" contains a series of thumbnail sketches of the families of catfish with, among other things, characteristics that help to distinguish each. In order

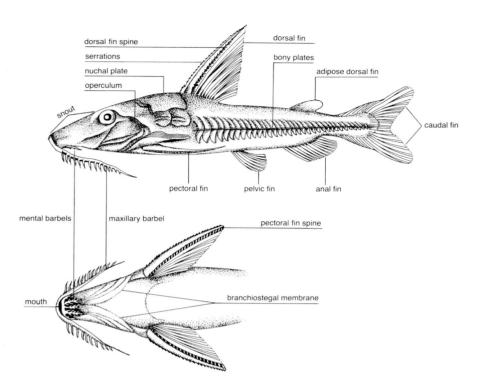

Some features of catfishes that are used for purposes of identification. *Illustration redrawn from:* Eigenmann, 1925.

to place catfishes properly into families, it is first necessary to have a basic understanding of the anatomical features of catfishes that are used for identification purposes. The following brief survey covers the external features that are used to distinguish catfish families.

All aspects of the anatomy of fishes are described in relation to certain standard directions. The uppermost part of the fish is said to be dorsal, the lower part ventral; the mouth end is anterior, and the tail end is posterior, or caudal. Thus, in catfishes, the fin situated behind the top of the head, which usually contains a strong spine, is the dorsal fin, and the dorsal fin spine is located at the anterior edge of

that fin. Usually a second, fleshy fin is found just posterior to the dorsal fin; it is called the adipose dorsal fin or adipose fin. "Adipose" is the term for tissues that store fat, and the adipose fin usually consists of adipose cells instead of rays. In some catfishes, however, the adipose dorsal fin can have one or more bony structures that help give the fin shape.

The fin at the tail is termed the caudal fin. Along the ventral midline of the body is the anal fin, and just anterior to that fin is a pair of fins called the pelvic fins, or ventral fins. Finally, one additional pair of fins, the pectoral fins, are located just behind the head. The first ray of the pectoral fin, and sometimes the pelvic fin, is thickened and enlarged, forming a fin spine. In some catfishes the pectoral fin spine is replaced by a threadlike, or filamentous, ray.

The spines of the pectoral and dorsal fins can either be smooth on the surface or covered with projections or ridges. Spines covered by sharp or pointed projections are said to be serrated. The presence or absence and the location of serrations are widely used to distinguish species that may otherwise be quite similar in appearance.

The head of catfishes can be divided into several regions. The area

Pseudacanthicus sp., the flame pleco. Note the scutes that completely cover the body. *Photo by:* P. Loiselle.

anterior to the eye is called the snout This area contains the nostrils and, i present, the nasal barbels. There are two nostrils on each side of the head anterior and posterior. These may be quite close together so that they seem to be one structure, separated by only a small flap of skin, or they may be separated by a large area of skin. The distance between the nostrils is ofter crucial in the identification of a fish a the level of family.

Behind the head dorsally is the nu chal region, which would correspond to the neck if fishes had necks. In mos catfishes it can be described as the region between the back of the skull and the beginning of the dorsal fin. In this location many catfishes have either a long, thin projection, called the supraoccipital spine, that extends backward from the skull or a bony plate, called the nuchal plate, that sits between the skull and the dorsal fin The presence, size, and shape o these two bones are often used in the

The tail end of *Pterodoras angeli,* showing the single row of scutes that runs along the body of this and all other members of the family Doradidae. *Photo by:* C. Ferraris.

identification of various catfish families.

A movable operculum is found on either side of the nuchal region, just ahead of the pectoral fins. The operculum covers the gills and is open ventrally, allowing water that has passed through the gill filaments to leave the gill cavity. The operculum is connected like a trap door; it can be pushed open by the force of the expelled water, but it is pulled close at all other times. The operculum is attached along the ventral surface of the head by a flap of skin called the branchiostegal membrane. Often the point of attachment is just behind the lower jaw, and the gill can be seen easily if the operculum is gently pushed to the side. In some catfishes, however, the operculum and branchiostegal membrane are broadly joined to the ventral surface of the fish's body so that the gill cannot be seen from below the fish, and only a small opening is left through which water is expelled. This is usually referred to as "united gill membranes" and is widely used in the identification of catfish to the level of family. For example, all doradids, auchenipterids, and centromochlids have united gill membranes, while pimelodids, bagrids, and ictalurids don't, instead having what are generally called "free" gill membranes.

The body of catfishes is usually covered with thick skin and is always without true scales. Some groups of catfishes have one or more series of overlapping bony plates covering part or all of the body. The structure of these plates is sufficiently different from typical scales in structure and growth to warrant giving them a sepa-

Parancistrus auranticus, with clusters of odontodes on the cheek and the pectoral spine. *Photo by:* M. Smith.

rate name. Unlike the scales of most fishes, the bony armor of catfishes cannot be removed easily from the fish without causing serious injury. The shape and arrangement of these plates are useful for identification (for example, all members of the family Doradidae have a single row of plates along the sides of the body). In some species the plates are quite small except for those near the tail. In other species the plates are uniformly large, even to the point of covering the entire sides of the body. Members of the families Loricariidae and Callichthyidae are so completely covered with plates that they are quite often referred to as "armored catfishes."

The body surfaces of members of several families of catfishes are covered with small stiff bristles called odontodes. These odontodes are really teeth that develop just below the surface of the skin. The location of these bristles is characteristic of several groups of fishes; for example, all loricariids and callichthyids have extremely fine odontodes covering the surface of all of their body armor and their fin spines. Some loricariids, especially bristle nose cats (genus *Ancistrus*), *Panaque,* and their relatives, also have a discrete patch of larger odontodes at the sides of their head, just in front of their opercles. These opercular odontodes are attached to the underlying bones in such a manner that they can be splayed out.

The head of every catfish has one or more pairs of threadlike projections, called barbels. These barbels are located someplace around the mouth and are covered with taste buds quite similar to those found on the surface of your tongue. A barbel may be a simple, soft, whiplike structure, or it may have a row of smaller barbels branching off from it. Sometimes the base of a barbel has a flap of skin that gives the impression that the barbel is stout at the base. The skin flaps of all the barbels around the mouth can be joined together to form a flexible tube around the mouth. Catfishes with this structure can be seen vacuuming the sand at the bottom of the tank, picking up food and sand.

The location of barbels is very important in identifying catfishes. All catfishes have at least one pair of barbels at or slightly above the angle of the mouth. This maxillary barbel is often the largest, and sometimes the only, barbel found. In some members of the family Pimelodidae the maxillary barbel may be longer than the fish itself, and the tip may trail well behind the swimming fish. At the other extreme, the maxillary barbel in species of the auchenipterid genus *Ageneiosus* is only slightly larger than the eye and is hidden in a fold of skin, making it almost impossible to see. *Corydoras* and its relatives have a second barbel just at the base of the maxillary barbel. This is called the rictal barbel. In most catfishes one or two pairs of barbels are found on the chin, either just below the lower lip or farther back, under the head. These mental barbels are usually much shorter than the maxillary barbel, and one or both pairs are absent in some species. In the long-tailed banjo catfishes, however, several additional pairs of mental barbels can be seen extending down to the belly of the fish.

One last pair of barbels is sometimes found on the snout, between the upper lip and the eye. This is called the nasal barbel, as it is associated with either the anterior or posterior nostril. Many catfishes lack nasal barbels,

and in some the barbel is so small that seeing it in a living fish requires a close look.

Although there is much more to the anatomy of catfishes, only one additional catfish part will be mentioned here. The eyes of catfishes are often involved in the process of identifying these fishes. The size and placement of eyes on the head can be quite different even in closely related species. Two commonly used measures of eye size are important to know. The first is the size of the eye in comparison to the length of the snout (the snout is defined as the area from the upper jaws to the beginning of the eye). Small eyes or eyes set far back

Elongated opercular odontodes are found in adult males of some loricariids, such as this *Panaque* sp. *Photo by:* C. Ferraris.

on the head will be insignificant in comparison to the snout. Large or anteriorly placed eyes may exceed the snout in size. In a similar fashion, the distance between the eyes can be measured. The ratio between the size of the eye and the shortest distance between them (called the interorbital distance) is used to help distinguish species. A good example of this is in some species of armored suckermouth catfishes. The panaques and Andes plecos (genus *Chaetostoma*) have very widely spaced eyes and a large interorbital distance. Although the sailfin plecos (genus *Pterygo-*

plichthys) also have smallish eyes, the interorbital distance is quite noticeably less.

One final note about eyes is in order: the eyes of some species of armored suckermouth catfish have a peculiar flap on the iris that extends over the pupil. A friend of mine refers to this as an "omega eye," in reference to the U-shaped remainder of the black pupil. Species of plecos that are otherwise quite similar in appearance can be told apart by the presence or absence of an omega eye, and it is well worth looking for if you have not yet noticed it.

This large pimelodid, *Pinirhampus pirinampu,* shows the typical arrangement of barbels surrounding the mouth in catfish. *Photo by:* C. Ferraris.

The new royal *Panaque*, an
unnamed species. *Photo by:* P.
Loiselle.

*Pterygoplichthys gibbiceps. Photo
by:* C. Ferraris.

Peckoltia pulcher, showing interopercular odontodes and the omega eye. *Photo by:* M. Smith.

Unlike members of the genus *Peckoltia*, members of the genus *Hypostomus*, such as the one shown here, lack interopercular odontodes. *Photo by:* M. Smith.

Keeping Catfishes in the Aquarium

With the great diversity of form and habits characterizing the more than 2500 species of catfishes, there is likely to be at least one species that would fit into any conceivable aquarium situation. The key to success, then, is to match catfish and aquarium.

I think of catfishes as being divisible into five classes of aquarium residents, based on the fish keeper's interests and the setups required. Unquestionably, a species of catfish can fall into more than one category, but this classification will provide some general ideas of how to handle a catfish once you have established a role for it. The discussion below emphasizes various aquarium conditions and the kinds of catfishes that are suitable for each.

Community Catfishes

Most catfishes kept at present belong to the first class, which I call, simply, community fishes. These are catfishes that are added to a community tank to provide an increase in diversity and beauty. A large number of fishes can be considered appropriate members of an aquarium community, and in my opinion no community tank is complete without catfish. Almost every freshwater lake or stream in the world has some catfishes. And although catfish rarely if ever come to mind when thinking about the beauty of coral reefs, members of two families can be

Ageneiosus magoi, a catfish with a big appetite and a comparable mouth. *Photo by:* C. Ferraris.

commonly seen in these breathtaking environments.

In community aquaria a catfish can be either a prominent, highly visible member of the tank or a cryptic member that rarely shows itself, even at feeding time. I find the latter among the most enjoyable of catfishes. True, you may not be able to see the fish on demand, but instead you are treated to an unexpected and pleasant surprise when the fish finally makes its appearance.

While catfish are obvious candidates for inclusion in community aquaria, the choice of which catfish to include is not so simple. Most guides to fish keeping comment on the need to maintain catfish in communities that contain only fishes that are too large to be swallowed. While this is a good general rule of thumb, it overlooks two important considerations: first, there are many catfishes that are not predatory and can readily be included with smaller fishes; second, predatory fishes grow, so a catfish that once was small enough to be included in a community tank may soon outgrow the community and become a predator. This is a special problem with nocturnal or shy catfishes, which may disappear into the rockwork for weeks or months at a time, only to reappear much enlarged. This is all too commonly seen with members of the family Ariidae, the so-called shark cats. These fishes are usually purchased at a very small size and placed in community tanks with a variety of small to medium-sized fishes. For a while they blend in well with the other fishes, but eventually they disappear from sight. These cute little catfishes soon become quite large, at the expense of many of the other aquarium residents, which one by one mysteriously disappear.

Shark cats are not alone in this. Quite a number of pimelodid catfishes that are imported at a small and very

Even this full, most individuals of *Ageneiosus magoi* would attempt to eat another goldfish if given the chance. *Photo by:* C. Ferraris.

This and virtually all other species of *Corydoras* are perfect candidates for community aquaria. *Photo by:* C. Ferraris.

attractive size later demonstrate their voracious feeding habits. Sadly, one of the most attractive species of South American pimelodid catfishes, the angelicus cat (*Pimelodus pictus*), belongs to this group. Although it never gets large enough to be a serious threat to many species, it is more than happy to feed on neons and a number of smaller tetras that would otherwise contribute to an attractive South American community aquarium. Other species that must be considered carefully when setting up a small community aquarium include the slender pimelodellas, the large-headed *Pseudopimelodus* species, and the sailfin pimelodids of the genus *Leiarius*. Species of a number of other families also warrant caution. North American ictalurids, especially the commonly sold channel cat, *Ictalurus punctatus,* and most of the African and Asian bagrid catfishes can quickly outgrow their welcome in most community aquaria.

I am not advocating that these fishes not be kept in community aquaria. Indeed, they should be. But the aquarium must be closely monitored, and when the catfish outgrows the remaining fishes in the aquarium, it is time to move it to another home. This may require paying close attention to the numbers of other fish in the aquarium. If the numbers decrease without reason, suspect a catfish.

Another important consideration in keeping catfish in community aquaria is that most often they are bottom residents, and nocturnal besides. Any food meant for these catfishes must first pass through the water column (and the scrutiny of all the midwater residents of the tank) and then remain uneaten at least until after the lights are turned out and the catfishes become active. If the food doesn't survive that long, the catfishes will either go without, and eventually starve, or alter their feeding habits: they will become "worker" fishes (discussed

27

Pseudodoras niger, the dolphin catfish, grows too large for all but public aquaria. *Photo by:* C. Ferraris.

later), scavenging for food, or possibly more active predators. Neither of these options is suited to the proper maintenance of a community aquarium, and every effort should be made to avoid the necessity of this change.

A variety of catfishes are appropriate for small community aquaria. Most popular are species of *Corydoras,* and rightfully so. Corys, almost without exception, are peaceful, active fishes that tolerate a range of aquarium conditions. They complement a wide range of community aquarium themes and are rarely if ever problematic. Some species that have recently become available are more restricted in their tolerance of tank conditions and may not be suitable for community aquaria. These species are usually more expensive and less readily found—two good indications that they do not belong in community situations.

Most of the available doradid species are also appropriate community fishes. They tend to be more secretive than corys, but are generally quite peaceful and tolerant. Of the species that can often be found, only a few (*Pterodoras granulosus,* sometimes called the "prehistoric cat," and *Pseudodoras niger,* the "dolphin cat") grow too large for most community aquaria. Many species of the African upside-down cats of the genus *Synodontis* can also be included in community aquaria. These tend to be even less outgoing than doradids, but do make occasional appearances and are quite graceful swimmers. Auchenipterids and centromochlids are both good candidates for community aquaria. Nearly all species in each of these families remain small enough to be longtime residents in average-sized tanks, and most species are reasonably peaceful if kept well fed. Members of both of these families show an interesting behavior that adds to their appeal. Although bottom dwellers that spend much of their time out of sight, they can quickly react to food and quite promptly head upward to feed at the surface. There, they gracefully cruise from end to end searching for floating bits of food. Unfortunately, most species of these families are not readily available, and one of the most available is an exception to this generally favorable view. Wood cats, which go by the scientific name *Trachelyopterus* (often listed in the literature as *Parauchenipterus* or *Trachycorystes*), are exceedingly retiring and, more important, can be voracious predators. These fishes must be kept with comparatively large tankmates.

Armored suckermouth catfish, family Loricariidae, are among the most widely kept community catfish. As they are primarily herbivorous, there is little reason for concern about any of these fishes consuming tankmates. This is not to say that loricariids can be added indiscriminately to community aquaria. Many species are quite territorial and cannot always be placed in a tank that

contains either another member of the species (called a conspecific) or another loricariid. This seems especially true of ancistrine loricariids, those that have large opercular odontodes. Many of these species seem to require extremely large territories and will not tolerate an intruding individual. Even some relatively small species, such as the many attractive clown plecos belonging to the genus *Peckoltia,* cannot be kept together without surprisingly large aquaria.

Community catfishes are not restricted to bottom dwellers only. Midwater swimmers such as the glass catfishes (family Siluridae), iridescent sharks (Pangasiidae), and the debauwi cat and its relatives (family Schilbidae) can be added to many community tanks. However, many of the midwater swimming catfishes do

Eutropiellus buffei (shown here) and its congener *E. debauwi* are among the most attractive midwater catfishes. *Photo by:* P. Loiselle.

29

best in schools of six or more individuals. Smaller groups and especially individual fishes tend to be shy, retiring to the far corners of tanks (instead of being out and about where they can be enjoyed), and quite often dying shortly thereafter. Many species of schilbids and silurids remain relatively small and can be kept in small community tanks. In contrast, even the smallest pangasiid, *Pangasius sutchi*, grows quickly from the 1- to 2-inch fish that is most commonly available to a size of 12 inches or more, thereby requiring a different home. Although armored catfishes are generally thought of as bottom dwellers, two species of the callichthyid genus *Dianema*, the porthole cats, spend much of their time swimming, or at least hovering, in the water column. Of these, the flag-tailed porthole cat, *D. urostriata*, is one of the most attractive members and

Unlike nearly all other armored catfishes, the two species of *Dianema* spend most of their time swimming in midwater. *Photo by:* P. Loiselle.

an excellent addition to community aquaria. Among the ever-popular *Corydoras*, several smaller species, including *C. pygmaeus*, *C. habrosus*, and *C. hastatus*, also seem at home in midwater, especially in groups. These pygmy corys are especially suitable for very small community aquaria.

Worker Catfishes

The second class is what I call working catfish: a fish that is supposed to help keep an aquarium clean or a fish added to clean up a dirty tank. It seems that early in the history of catfish keeping, catfishes in general acquired a reputation as cleaners, and now many new aquarists seem to think that all catfishes are good at keeping the bottom of the tank clean. That couldn't be further from the truth. More often than not, catfish contribute very little to the cleanliness of an aquarium, and they are not usually good scavengers. When they do scavenge the bottom of the tank for food,

At least three small species of *Corydoras,* including *C. habrosus* (shown here), are midwater swimmers. *Photo by:* J. O'Malley.

it is often a sign that they are not being properly fed and are trying to keep from starving to death. This is not to say that catfishes are not useful in maintaining a clean aquarium. Instead, it is important to know that not all catfishes can function that way, and those that can help clean an aquarium do so in specific ways. No working catfish can be expected to clean all types of dirty aquaria.

There are two main ways in which catfishes can participate in tank maintenance and cleaning: they can either remove unwanted algae from the glass and rockwork or remove excess food that resulted from overfeeding other fishes in the aquarium. Algae cleaning has traditionally been the responsibility of a loach called the "Chinese algae eater" (*Gyrinocheilus* spp.). When first purchased, Chinese algae eaters are often quite good at this task. They often become aggressive, however, and can quickly outgrow their tank—and their welcome. On the other hand, a large number of catfishes are equal to the task of algae

cleaning and are also quite attractive additions to the community aquarium. Most of these catfishes are members of the Neotropical family Loricariidae, the whiptail catfishes and their relatives. Loricariids are unusual among catfishes by being vegetarian, for the most part. Algae forms the bulk of their diets in nature, and it is often readily eaten in aquaria. Like most herbivorous animals, algae-eating catfishes need a lot of food, and the volumes required to keep even a single catfish well fed usually exceed the algae production in an aquarium. Either the diet of the working catfish must be supplemented with other vegetable matter (see under "Food" in the chapter "The Catfish Aquarium") to make up the difference or, often the better solution, the working catfish must be moved from aquarium to aquarium when the amount of algae decreases.

When in doubt it is always a good idea to provide new loricariid catfishes, such as this magnificent zebra peckoltia, with an abundance of vegetable matter for food. *Photo by:* M. Smith.

Supplemental feeding is not bad for the fish and, in fact, can provide a better balance of nutrients. The problem is that loricariids seem to learn very quickly that the supplemental food is routinely available and there is no need to graze the algae. Once these fishes stop grazing, it is difficult to convince them to return to it, and a worker fish has been lost. At this point it is necessary to obtain another fish to remove tank algae. This transition from worker to nonworker is often avoided by not allowing them to begin supplemental feeding and giving them access only to algae. But maintaining a worker catfish does take some effort and attention. The algae levels in the tank must be closely monitored and

the worker removed to another tank when the food supply is insufficient. It is important, of course, that the newly targeted tank be similar in water chemistry and temperature to the aquarium from which the worker is being transferred, so as not to shock the fish.

The species of catfish that is chosen for algae-cleaning duty depends a great deal on the size and number of aquaria the same fish can be used for. Small species belonging to any of a number of genera, such as *Peckoltia, Lasiancistrus, Chaetostoma,* or smaller whiptails (for example, *Rineloricaria*), are best for aquaria of less than thirty gallons. In addition, small individuals of larger species are appropriate for these smaller aquaria. Even for somewhat larger tanks, a couple of individuals of small species may be preferable to a single larger individual. In substantially larger aquaria these small species often cannot keep up with algae production and must be replaced by larger species of loricariids. Species of *Panaque,* such as the blue-eye or the exquisite royal, are suitable if your budget permits. There are even larger species, such as *Pterygoplichthys gibbiceps*; *P. anisiti* (the snow king) and several species of *Hypostomus* can be used for the largest of home aquaria. As this section of the book is being written, many spectacular species of loricariids that have never before been seen in the American tropical fish trade are appearing at the importers' warehouses and in pet stores. Several of these may become readily available and be the "cleaner" catfish of the future.

The second type of worker fish, one that cleans up the uneaten food in community aquaria, is somewhat harder to categorize. As stated above, almost all catfishes will scavenge as an alternative to starving, but that's not to say that forcing a catfish to scavenge is an acceptable way to treat any catfish. Few species of catfishes are true scavengers in nature. Species of *Corydoras* and their relatives are perhaps best known for this activity. Corys are often seen with their snouts burrowing through the surface of the gravel or sand substrate, stopping at intervals to ingest a particularly large morsel of food. Few other catfishes are similarly able to glean food from the substrate. Some members of the Doradidae, especially the mouse cats or zipper cats, have the ability to vacuum up sand and detritus, sift out the edible portions, and eject the rest back into the water. Few other catfishes seem to exhibit an equivalent

Because of their small adult size, most species of *Peckoltia* are quite suitable additions to even the smallest of aquaria. *Photo by:* A. van den Nieuwenhuizen.

Although they are suitable for small aquaria when young, this *Pterygoplichthys gibbiceps* and most other species of that genus quickly outgrow any tank smaller than 55 gallons in volume. *Photo by:* P. Loiselle.

zeal for sand sifting when other food is available.

If a catfish is incorporated into a fish community as a worker, it is important to monitor its health regularly (which is sometimes difficult to do with nocturnal doradids) to be sure that adequate amounts of food are available. A fish that does not appear to grow or that shows signs of emaciation and loss of activity may not be obtaining enough food and should no longer be treated as a worker.

Pet Catfishes

The third category of aquarium catfishes is what can be called pet fish. By this I mean fish that respond to their owners' approach, often by com-

ing to the surface or even partially out of the water to allow themselves to be touched. Generally this happens only with relatively large catfishes, and members of some families seem more likely candidates than others. Many species of the Neotropical family Pimelodidae are kept in this manner. The South American red-tailed cat (*Phractocephalus*) and sailfin pimelodids (*Leiarius* and *Perrunichthys*), along with the African giraffe cat (*Auchenoglanis*) of the family Bagridae, are especially adaptable to this. They seem to be trained quickly (or is it they that do the training?) to respond to the approach of anyone, especially if a food reward follows. Some of these large catfish live for years (no one knows for sure how long) and can quickly become a member of the family. More often than not, fishes intended to be pet catfish are obtained at a small size (at present, all of these fishes are wild caught and shipped to the United States). With tender loving care they can grow quickly and then require a larger home. For many species of Pimelodidae, this process may need to be repeated over and over again, with requisite rearrangement of the fish room or family room to accommodate the ever-larger replacement aquarium. The increasing size and gentle temperament of these pet catfish can easily make them the center of attraction. But large catfish, like any large pet, require an ever-increasing food supply and maintenance. This is especially important to consider at the beginning stages of keeping a pet catfish. Providing small individuals with goldfish treats or even a staple of goldfish may not cost a lot of money, but as the fish grow in size, so does the goldfish bill. The fish may be reluctant to switch to a less expensive or more readily available source of food, such as pellets.

Oddball Catfishes

A fourth class of catfishes can be called novelty or oddball catfishes—

those that are, in the eye of their keeper, sufficiently unusual to warrant being kept in special conditions. This is probably the most personalized class of fishes, with each fish keeper having a different idea of what constitutes a novelty fish. Due to differences in import-export patterns, an oddball in one part of the country may be a common fish somewhere else. There are some species that, because of their appearance, would probably be considered oddballs no matter how abundant they are: the frogmouth catfish (*Chaca*), electric cat (*Malapterurus*), and long-tailed banjo catfishes come to mind. Before they were banned from the United States, albino walking catfish (*Clarias batrachus*) were very popular as a novelty. Many pet shops would display one of these fishes for their unusual appearance and albi-

At 5 inches this juvenile tiger shovel nose catfish (genus *Pseudoplatystoma*) makes an attractive, novel addition to an aquarium. *Photo by:* J. O'Malley.

35

nism. No matter how often you saw them, their peculiar appearance set them apart. Oddballs are usually given aquaria of their own, and often for good reason. Many catfishes have voracious appetites (sometimes seemingly insatiable), and apparently small, unimposing fishes may have grand ideas about what they consider edible. It is best to experiment with an unknown oddball in a separate tank rather than put it in your favorite community aquarium.

Oddballs are frequently fishes that are discovered as "contaminants" in shipments of common catfish. Almost always, contaminants are similar to such commonly imported catfishes as corys and zamora cats. Virtually all examples of the imitator-pimelodids, genus *Brachyrhamdia,* were discovered in shipments of one or another

Tiger shovel nose catfishes grow to be quite a handful. This must be considered when deciding whether to purchase one for an aquarium. *Photo by:* P. Loiselle.

species of *Corydoras.* Specimens of *Brachyrhamdia* can often be found swimming in retailers' tanks.

Another source of oddballs is newly imported species. Whenever an exporter finds new habitats for fishes, they are bound to encounter species of fishes that were not previously marketed. As these fishes reach wholesalers and pet stores, they are quickly grabbed by fish enthusiasts looking for something different. Sometimes the enthusiasm for these previously unseen or rarely seen species is sufficient to encourage exporters to redouble their efforts to find additional specimens. In time this may lead to an oddball's becoming a commonly seen species. A good example of this is the panda cory (*Corydoras panda*). Only a year or two ago, pandas were among the most sought after (and most expensive) of all corys. Peruvian fish exporters tried to meet the demand for this species, and may have been too successful. Pandas became quite plentiful when exporters discovered

Brachyrhamdia imitator, the first of several species of that genus thought to closely resemble one or more species of *Corydoras.* Photo by: H. Hieronimus.

places where they are locally abundant, and this species is in the process of losing its status as a novelty fish.

Oddballs form the nucleus of the future of the catfish hobby. It is through the discovery of new and different species that we are able to find catfishes that are suitable to become pet fishes or even breeders. This initial filtering of species by advanced hobbyists who "discover" new candidates for aquarium keeping and try to maintain them leads to insights as to whether a species can be readily kept in aquaria and under what conditions. They learn about whether a fish may be safely kept in community aquaria (often the hard way, through the loss of some or all of the remaining members of the tank). As this information is passed around to hobbyists by way of articles in club magazines and newsletters, and through talks given at meetings, the popularity of different species waxes or wanes.

Breeder Catfishes

The fifth group in my scheme is fishes that are kept to be bred in aquaria. This has been a central focus of fish keeping in much of the aquarium fish hobby, but not so with catfishes. It seems that catfishes, with few exceptions, have been considered impossible to breed in captivity, and little effort has been put forth to disprove this. In recent years that attitude has changed somewhat, with remarkable results. Over the past few years evidence of captive spawnings has been reported for several families of catfishes that had never previously shown any indication of reproductive activity. Internal fertilization was suggested for auchenipterids decades ago, but only within the past few years has it been verified. Species in such diverse fami-

37

Many species of *Corydoras,* such as this *C. panda,* are greatly sought after and command high prices when first introduced into the hobby. *Photo by:* J. O'Malley.

lies as the African Mochokidae and the South American Aspredinidae have reproduced in aquarium conditions and provided us with the first information of the spawning behavior of these fishes.

This is not to say that aquarium spawnings of catfishes were unknown before recent times. Some species of callichthyid catfishes have been spawned in captivity for decades, and the reproductive behavior of these species has been reported in both the popular and scientific literature.

The diversity of forms that are exhibited by catfishes is further reflected in their reproductive and parental behavior. As we learn more of the reproductive biology of catfishes, we can only become more amazed at their diverse behaviors and dream of what further discoveries will be made. There are some limitations as to which

catfishes can be bred in captivity, but we're a long way from needing to be seriously concerned about that.

In general, catfishes that are intended as breeders require special attention in a number of ways. Often they are given a separate aquarium of a larger size than might otherwise be considered necessary. The location of the tank can be important to control a number of factors, such as temperature (if individual tanks are not heated), human traffic, and height (if observation of the spawning behavior is important; no one wants to stand on a stepladder for hours watching the spawning behavior of fishes that were placed in a tank that was just a little too high to view comfortably). If the spawnings of these fishes have previously been reported, the tank should be designed to meet the needs of the fishes. For example, many species of *Corydoras* deposit eggs on plants, and for them a heavily planted tank would be valuable, if not a prerequisite to induce spawning. *Ancistrus* and many other loricariids spawn under overhanging structures or inside hollowed-out logs. Without an equivalent structure (which may be as simple as half a flower pot tipped on its side or a piece of PVC pipe), spawning these fishes is quite unlikely. However, because many catfishes that are available now have never been spawned in captivity, the requirements for these fishes are unknown. Although it is sometimes possible to make an educated guess at the spawning strategy of a given fish, based on available information about its native habitat, the spawning behavior of similar species, and so forth, a trial-and-error method is almost always necessary to determine the minimum acceptable conditions for these fish. At least two approaches are possible for this. The fish may be placed in a large aquarium with a range of habitats; for example, one side of the tank may be heavily planted and the other have a rockwork or submerged wood substrate. The pair can then choose from among the possibilities, assuming that at least one is suitable. This scheme will work best with small species for which a large enough tank can be employed. For larger species, or for aquarists who do not have the luxury of overly large aquaria, a second plan is needed. Instead of having a choice of habitats in a single aquarium, the potential spawners may be placed in a single-theme aquarium. After a period of time the theme can be changed, until a successful spawning has been achieved.

Keeping catfishes for breeding can be thought of in two ways: either the catfishes are kept primarily for the purpose of making more catfishes or they are kept for observation of their reproductive and parenting behaviors. Most aquarists are more interested in the former, which I will discuss after first touching briefly on the latter.

Watching fishes spawn and guard their young can be one of the most rewarding facets of the aquarium hobby. Catfishes in general seem to exhibit a higher degree of parental care than do many other fishes kept in aquaria, and may well rival the much better known cichlids in the effort they expend in caring for their eggs and young. Unfortunately, unlike many cichlids, catfishes are quite secretive about their brood care, and special efforts must be made to be able to observe reproductive activities. In addition to a suitable habitat for the pair, extra consideration must be given to the design of the tank to maximize the possibility of the spawning's taking place in a location that is at least partially visible. For cave- or hole-spawning catfishes, this is especially challenging, but it can usually be accomplished by orienting caves (either natural rockwork or clay pots or pipe) so that one opening is pointing toward the front of the aquarium. This is, of course, a bit of a trade-off. By increasing the probability of being able to observe a spawning, you may be decreasing the likelihood of the catfishes' being willing to spawn. The same can be said of observing parenting behavior. Those catfishes that show postspawning defensive behaviors—that is, tending and guarding of the nest and, later, the larvae—may be more parental when other fishes are in the aquarium. Thus, to really appreciate the extent to which parents will defend their young, it may be a valuable exercise to attempt to induce spawning in an aquarium containing other fishes; it may be necessary to introduce one or more fishes into a tank in which a pair of catfishes recently spawned. The potential problems in either of these alternatives should be quite obvious. While parental guarding behavior may be increased, it may not be sufficient to dissuade the intruder, thereby causing the loss of the spawn and possibly damage to the parents. On the other hand, the parents may more than meet the challenge of the intruding fish and cause it serious injury. These problems can be minimized by taking precautions that are associated with the introduction of any two combative fishes to each other.

If observing the behaviors associated with catfish reproduction is of secondary importance, the job of the aquarist is simplified in many ways. Concern must still be given to providing appropriate environmental conditions for the species that are to be spawned, but the rigors of providing conditions that are both adequate for the fish and suitable for observation are eliminated. Location of the aquarium is less important when observations will not be made, but it is still critically important to be able to see the tank so that decisions can be made about the fry when the fishes have spawned.

Typically, the first spawning of a catfish species invokes a series of standard questions that have to be addressed, many as soon as the spawn is noticed. Should the eggs be separated from the parents or left as is? If separated, which is better, to remove the parents or the eggs? Under what conditions should the eggs be maintained? How long before the eggs hatch? What should the newly hatched fishes be fed? And so on. All of these questions address the basic question of whether the aquarist or the fish are better parents for the newly deposited eggs, and which set of parents will increase the probability of the eggs hatching successfully and provide the necessary care for the newly hatched catfish. Unfortunately, there is no set answer for this dilemma, and aquarists I know all seem to take different approaches.

There are distinct advantages both to leaving parents and offspring together and to removing one or the other, at least in certain situations. Separating the parents from the eggs guarantees that the eggs aren't eaten (assuming no other fishes are in the aquarium), and removing the eggs may allow for easier observation of the development of the eggs and larvae. Losses of eggs or larvae will be noticed quite quickly, and steps can be taken to avert further attrition. Keeping eggs and parents (or parent) together may provide an element to rearing the young that might not otherwise be considered important. For example, the Asian bagrid *Mystus gulio* feeds its young with secretions from its belly skin; in the absence of the parents, it may not be possible to provide an acceptable alternative food source for the newly hatched young. In addition, parental activity is sometimes needed to ensure successful hatching of the eggs. For example, some whiptail suckermouth catfish eggs need to be punctured by the guarding male before the young can break out of their embryonic home.

To breed a species of catfish, a number of obstacles must first be overcome. The onset of maturity is not always evident, and because many catfishes do not exhibit a great degree of sexual dimorphism (see the chapter "Reproduction"), knowing whether the target fishes are mature is often problematical. I have seen a number of instances where aquarists thought they had sexually mature fish that were months if not years away from adulthood. In the same regard, the virtual absence of sexual dimorphism in some species can frustrate aquarists who may be keeping two (or more) individuals of the same sex in a breeding tank and wondering why nothing happens. Equally frustrating is the possibility that two similar catfishes may not be of the same species. Subtle differences that may be interpreted as sexual dimorphism or just individual variation may in fact represent differences between species. This seems to be a special problem for South American catfishes, for a couple of reasons. Many shipments from South America have mixed-species lots that are sold to dealers as a single species. These fishes often come to the exporters from a number of different localities and are combined into lots for convenience in packing and shipping. As a number of South American catfish species seem to be quite restricted in their ranges, the fishes of these different localities may well represent different species. Unless the importers or wholesalers recognize the differences, they may sell the fishes as one species, and the problem is passed on to the aquarist. Even with the burgeoning amount of literature on catfish identification that has become available recently, the distinction between similar species may not yet be recorded, leaving an interested hobbyist to guess whether fishes that seem slightly different actually are part of a single species.

Because the art of breeding catfishes is still in its infancy, many mistakes will be made for every success that is finally recorded. But learning from mistakes is as much a part of the aquarium hobby as it is of all other aspects of life. Sharing mistakes with others may prevent them from making the same ones, so that eventually someone will hit upon the correct formula for inducing the spawning of yet another catfish.

The pimelodid *Goeldiella eques.* *Photo by:* M. Smith.

Handling Catfishes

Caring for the Catfish

Once placed in a good home, most catfishes will be content to remain in the aquarium almost indefinitely. In general, it is in the best interests of both the catfish and the aquarist to leave well enough alone and not move fish unnecessarily; however, circumstances may dictate that a catfish be moved from one aquarium to another.

The first move necessarily happens when a new acquisition is brought home and placed in a temporary quarantine tank before moving into its "permanent" home. More than one aquarist has brought home a cute little catfish to add to a community tank

The scutes of loricariids (such as this *Hemiancistrus landoni*) and doradids can become entangled quickly in the mesh of many dip nets. *Photo by:* P. Loiselle.

only to find later that the fish has outgrown the aquarium, and perhaps eaten all of the other residents in the process. Other times a move may be dictated by outside forces, such as a leaking aquarium seal.

Sometimes, of course, moves are made by design, not necessity. Breeding stock can be put together in a "spawning" tank and later removed to protect the parents or brood. Trades and purchases of new specimens all require moves, and so does the transport of a prized individual to and from a fish show.

Whatever the reason, moving catfish safely requires a bit of technique to ensure the well-being of both the fish and the handler. As mentioned earlier, almost all catfishes have at least one spine somewhere on their body. Sometimes the spines are enveloped in a toxin (more on this later), but the spine(s) alone should be rea-

son enough to pay particular care when handling these fishes.

Dip nets, although commonly used to catch and transfer fishes in aquaria, fare poorly with many catfishes. Nets with large mesh usually get entangled with spines or scutes as the fish struggles to extricate itself. As the struggle continues, the fish becomes more enmeshed. Often, the fastest and safest way to extract a fish from this situation is to cut the net, a proposition that soon becomes prohibitively expensive. Fine-mesh nets, with holes too small to allow catfish spines to penetrate, are much more appropriate for catfish catching. Even these nets are subject to an occasional snag, but much less frequently than are coarser nets.

Alternatively, catfishes can be captured with a plastic or glass container and transferred in water to another aquarium. This has the advantage of keeping the fish wet at all times and is truly snag-free, but it requires a bit of practice, or luck, to persuade a fish to enter the container. This technique is especially useful when transferring delicate or sick fishes, in order to minimize the stress of a transfer.

Many nocturnal catfishes, especially the doradids, auchenipterids, and centromochlids, will aggressively remain in rockwork, wood crevices, or plastic (PVC) tubing against all efforts to remove them. This characteristic makes transferring them, tubing and all, easy so long as the final destination is large enough to accommodate both. If removing the fish is essential, keep in mind that forcible eviction rarely succeeds, especially with larger fishes. Attempts to dislodge fish seem only to exacerbate the problem; the fish "digs in" and becomes immovable to any effort short of breaking its spines. Generally, however, you can coax a fish out by suspending its hiding place out of the water, with the opening pointing downward, just above a waiting net or tank. After a while the fish will yield to gravity and drop to the container below. The relatively short stay out of water seems not to harm it.

A large catfish creates special problems in handling. A net that covers just the front end of the fish is of little use, and a water-laden container that is big enough to enclose such a fish will be too heavy to move. About the only solution is to reach in and grab the fish— something that should be done only with adequate preparation. Any fish too large to capture with a net is likely to be stronger than you would expect. A careless grab at such a fish will do little to immobilize it; more likely, it will result in a handful of unwanted scrapes (and pain). Simultaneously pinning down the tail and the head, keeping all fingers in front of the pectoral spines, will effectively immobilize most fish. Covering the eyes of the fish with the palm of the hand that is grasping the head often helps to keep the fish calm during the move. Sometimes a towel or other dense cloth placed over the fish will provide a better grip and lessen the chance of the handler being scraped or stabbed.

Of course, getting a catfish out of an aquarium is only the first problem to be overcome. Transporting catfishes comes with its own set of problems. Short moves of a few feet to a few miles can be accomplished safely with little more than a plastic pail. (Pails with covers are frequently discarded by fast-food restaurants and delicatessens and can be used for a large number of aquarium-related activities. No serious fish keeper should be without several.) Only a few warnings are in order here. First, keep the container covered at all times. It takes a lot longer to find a replacement for a dried-out pet catfish than it does to find a cover for a bucket. Second, aerate the bucket for anything other than a very short move. Although most catfishes are able to withstand brief periods of reduced oxygen, any unnecessary stress should be avoided. If the move means transporting a fish in exceptionally hot or cold weather, it is best to use the largest container available with as much water as you can carry. Water is an excellent temperature buffer, and larger volumes will minimize the temperature fluctuations to which the fish will be subjected. Carrying a fish in a lot of water won't protect it from several hours in an unheated car during a snowstorm, but lots of water combined with common sense work well together. Third, think about what fishes are being moved. Large catfishes rarely travel well together. It makes little sense to move fishes if they end up so badly battered that there's little hope of recovery. While one to a pail may not always be feasible, even a short ill-considered pairing may be devastating.

Although catfishes are routinely sent across the country via mail or air freight, a dehydrated catfish and a soggy shipping container are the usual result of thoughtless attempts to ship them. The spines of all but the smallest catfish will readily penetrate many plastic bags. In addition, long confinement in total darkness seems to give catfish a green light to do battle. In either case, the recipient of the shipment is unlikely to be very enthusiastic about the newly acquired specimens.

The first problem can be solved in a number of ways. Double-bagging fish is a standard precaution to protect against leakage. A thick layer of newspaper between the bags, at least for the lower half, will further protect the fish in two ways: the newspaper will usually prevent catfish spines from going through both bags, but even if it doesn't, the soggy newspaper will keep the atmosphere inside the shipping container from drying out too quickly. Many catfishes will survive long periods out of water so long as their gills and skin remain moist and the temperature is within acceptable limits.

Keeping catfishes from injuring each other while in transit can be difficult or expensive or both. The best solution is to bag the specimens individually. When sending only a few fish, this is often not difficult, but as the number grows, so does the size of the container(s) needed, and the expense. There are a few ways to get around the need to individually bag fishes. Most important, with the exception of *Corydoras* and some of the more lethargic catfishes (such as banjos), fishes kept together should be of the same species and of approximately the same size. This seems to reduce the aggression of the largest ones, thereby keeping the smaller ones from being too badly damaged. In addition, it seems that placing only two fishes together in a bag is worse than having several together. With two, one usually comes out damaged, whereas larger numbers together tend not to fight.

I have heard about, but have not yet seen, cloth body bags used to keep individual fishes apart in one shipping container. The cloth bag constrains the fish, keeping spines and scutes from abrading others. Loosely woven bags would not seriously hinder the movement of water, thereby keeping

One of the most attractive species of armored suckermouth catfish is the recently imported gold nugget pleco. *Photo by:* M. Smith.

the fishes in about the same conditions as if they were moving about freely. In addition to protecting catfishes from each other, body bags would lessen the need to reinforce the plastic bags.

Making individual bags for fishes might seem to be a lot of work, especially if they are used infrequently, but an old sock is a simple alternative for many medium-sized catfishes. Put the fish in head first and quickly tie the open end to make a neat container with little effort. Removing the fish may require cutting it out of the bag carefully, but old socks always seem to be present, at least in my household.

A few additional considerations are in order when packing catfishes for transport. For short trips, a battery-operated air pump is generally sufficient to provide a source of air to any fish held in a bucket. Periods of confinement in sealed containers with a fixed amount of air require planning to ensure adequate oxygen for the entire journey. Most often, compressed oxygen is used in place of air to maximize

the time that the fishes can be confined. A large amount of air space filled with pure oxygen seems not to be detrimental to most catfishes but has lethal effects on others. The so-called air-breathing catfishes, such as the clariids and at least some callichthyids and loricariids, which routinely gulp a mouthful of air as an accessory source of oxygen, cannot live in high-oxygen environments for extended periods. Leaving these fishes in pure oxygen often results in their becoming disoriented, swimming erratically, and eventually succumbing. These fishes shouldn't be packed in oxygen but instead in either air or an air-oxygen mixture. If clean air is the chosen medium, then it is important to provide as much as possible to compensate for the lesser amount of oxygen present (20 percent is normal).

At times aquarists use chemicals to aid in the transportation of catfishes.

45

Two types of chemicals are used in this activity. One type conditions the water in which the fish are residing. Fishes being transported are usually confined in an exceptionally small quantity of water, which receives all of their waste products and retains them until the water is changed, usually at the end of the journey. This small volume of water tends not to have any of the substantial bacterial buildup common to well-established aquarium water (see under "Water Conditions" in "The Catfish Aquarium"). The combination of these two factors leads to the possibility of a buildup of exceedingly high concentrations of ammonia in the water, which can be harmful and even fatal to fishes. Water conditioners such as Amquel℠ reduce the buildup of ammonia and thus allow the catfishes to stay in the water longer.

The second type of chemical reduces the activity of the fish. Products such as Jungle's Hypno® keep most fishes calm while in transport, minimizing the damage a fish can inflict on itself and others. At the same time, a fish that is not hyperactive will release fewer waste products into the water.

Any of these chemicals must be used in accordance with the manufacturer's instructions. Overdoses can be harmful. Also, there have been a number of cases in which Hypno actually seemed to increase the activity of catfishes, at least for a while. This is, of course, the worst possible outcome of the use of such a chemical. If you intend to use one of these chemicals on a catfish for the first time, you might try it out in an aquarium one or more days before shipping and observe the fish's reaction. If an undesirable reaction occurs, you can remove the fish quickly, without subjecting it to prolonged exposure to the chemical.

Caring for the Catfish Handler

Handling catfishes can be a traumatic experience for the handler as well as the fish, if not done properly. Catfishes possess a formidable array of weapons that can make an encounter with them memorable, even painful.

The trio of spines that encircle the head of most catfish species cannot be overlooked whenever one contemplates touching one of these fishes, but there is a great amount of variation in the form of spines and how catfishes use them.

The spines of both the dorsal and pectoral fins of many catfishes can be locked open by a combination of ligaments and bones that act as a friction lock. When locked, these spines would break sooner than yield to force. Only the combination of muscle relaxation and the correct sequence of subtle movements of one or more bones can release the lock without damaging the spine. This means that a catfish can maintain the spines open without having to continually contract muscles, which might become fatigued and relax prematurely. The resulting array of spines means that any attempt by a predator to bite or grab one of these catfishes from above, in front, or either side will result in an encounter with one or more of these immovable spines. Among other things, any attempt to swallow a catfish whole (and I don't recommend that anyone try this!) must allow for the extra size necessary to engulf all three spines.

In addition, many catfish spines have a venom gland at their bases. The venom is produced in cells that are found along the surface of the bony spine (often in a groove or flattened surface along one side), near the tip. When the spine punctures tissues, venom cells burst from the pressure and the toxin is introduced into the wound, resulting in a reaction that varies from mild, like a bee sting, to life-threatening. Very little is known about the nature of the toxin, but many other fish venoms, which are proteins, are unstable in heat. According to leading experts in treating venomous animal stings, these fish toxins, and presumably those of catfishes as well, should be treated by soaking the affected limb (not just a single finger!) in water that is as hot as the victim can stand for thirty to ninety minutes. This should denature the toxin and relieve the pain, at least to some degree.

In general, spines come in three basic types. The first is a slender, straight spine with a needlelike point at the tip and sometimes a row of small recurved points, called serrae (as in serrated knife edges), along the front and hind margins but away from the tip. This is the most common type of spine and is found in a wide variety of catfish families. The point of this type of spine easily penetrates flesh with only a minimum of pressure. Catfishes that have this spine type cause the most painful stings. Although quite a number of species are armed with venomous spines, a few relatively common aquarium residents deserve special notice. The marine eel-tailed cat, *Plotosus lineatus,* has a well-deserved reputation for the strength of its toxin. Even at the commonly available size of one inch, this fish can cause a serious amount of pain. Likewise, the fossil cat, *Heteropneustes fossilis,* rightly deserves its other common name, "stinging cat," for the intensity of the pain caused by a puncture from its pectoral spine. Both of these fishes reportedly have caused

The slender, needlelike spines of the shovel nose catfish, *Sorubim lima,* can readily penetrate a handler's skin. *Photo by:* J. O'Malley.

Even a small doradid catfish, such as this *Acanthodoras cataphractus,* can cause a considerable amount of pain if it is allowed to clamp down on a finger. The milky-white fluid seen here is secreted by the catfish (see under "Problems" in the chapter "The Catfish Aquarium"). *Photo by:* C. Ferraris.

the death of affected individuals. Less dangerous, but painful nonetheless, are nearly all species of the family Pimelodidae, including such commonly available species as the angelicus cat (*Pimelodus pictus*). Especially painful are species of the genus *Pimelodella* and small specimens of the shovel nose cats, including *Sorubim lima* and *Sorubimichthys planiceps.* Even in North American waters, catfishes can cause quite a sting. Virtually all species of *Noturus,* the madtoms or stone cats, are reported to be able to give a nasty sting.

The second type of spine is more robust, usually with heavily serrated margins but not having a sharply pointed tip. This type of spine is found in doradids, auchenipterids, centromochlids, and aspredinids. All of these fishes, except the banjo cats, have a peculiar response to being picked up. Initially they extend their spines outward, as is done by all other catfishes. If they are still partially or wholly in a confined space, such as a hollowed-out log or piece of PVC pipe, they will firmly lodge themselves in place by this response, making it nearly impossible to remove them. If, on the other hand, they are grasped behind their pectoral fins, another response is invoked. Instead of extending their fin spines outward, they will clamp the pectoral spines close to their body. Anything caught between the body and spine will be scissored between the serrated inner surface of the spine and an often equally serrated cleithral bone that projects backward from behind the head. The force that these catfishes can generate to hold on is truly remarkable, and even a very small one can draw blood from a trapped finger. Only by keeping all your fingers in front of the pectoral spine base can you be sure that they are out of harm's way.

The third type of spine is bluntly rounded and densely covered with fine movable bristles (called odontodes). These spines are found in loricariids and some callichthyids (they are especially noticeable in adult males of *Dianema, Callichthys,* and *Hoplosternum*). These spines are robust and strong but are not pointed in such a way that they can penetrate skin; instead, the minute odontodes can have the same effect as sandpaper if one scrapes across the skin.

The spines that characterize catfishes are not the only potential source of injury to be considered when handling these fishes. The dermal scutes that are found in the armored catfishes are obvious reasons for concern. These scutes often have ridges that end in a sharp point posteriorly. An attempt to grab one of these fishes may result in a sore hand, especially if the fish isn't so firmly grasped that it is unable to swim away. The powerful tail of the larger species can add further injury by thrashing back and forth in an attempt to escape capture. Although no venoms are known to be associated with these body scutes, the

scrapes can become infected if not properly cleaned.

When considering the possibility of injury, one must not overlook the mouth. Although catfishes in general have small teeth, often closely resembling sandpaper, they have powerful jaws. This is most likely to be of concern only to people keeping larger pet fish that have been trained for hand feeding. Usually, by the time a pet fish has been trained to feed from the hand it has become quite used to the routine and will use only a minimum of effort to open and close its mouth. Even longtime pets can become spooked, though, and one that is spooked while feeding could quite easily clamp on to food and fingers with incredible force. Feeding such a fish requires paying undivided attention to the task, especially when it is being done by someone the fish is not used to seeing; slight differences in

Although the "gold seam" pleco (referring to the yellow border of the dorsal fin) is one of the largest of the spotted species, it is one of the easiest to keep in captivity. *Photo by:* P. Loiselle.

mannerisms may be interpreted incorrectly by the fish.

Finally, a discussion of problems facing a catfish handler would not be complete without a mention of the electric catfishes, genus *Malapterurus.* Electric cats are called "strong electric fishes" because of their ability to produce a substantial amount of electricity to either stun prey or ward off an unwanted intruder. The fish generate the electricity in an electric organ that is composed of modified muscle cells located just beneath the skin of nearly the entire length of the body. The addition of the electric organ to the underlying muscle is what gives these fish their peculiar sausagelike appearance. The electrical discharge consists of a rapid series of nearly instantaneous pulses of electricity that can be repeated almost 500 times per second. The whole discharge may continue for a full second and exceed 350 volts. The force of this discharge is generally not enough to cause any serious damage to an individual, but the shock caused by the sudden and often unexpected burst of electricity can cause a reflex action in the victim that may result in an injury. For example, a person may be so surprised by the shock received from even a small electric cat that he might jerk his hand out of the aquarium and hit it on a nearby piece of furniture or, worse, break a pane of aquarium glass in trying to remove his hand from the tank. Thus, the electric cat warrants extra caution during transfer from one tank to another and during aquarium cleanings. Contrary to popular thought, though, they are not always a serious threat and can be handled. Researchers on electric cat behavior have been able to pet their subjects without receiving any shock. If this is started with a small-sized individual, it is possible to make it a pet and hand-feed or handle it without being shocked. As with any animal, the key to success is making predictable movements so that the fish can learn and know what to expect. It is the unpredictable actions that usually cause fishes and other animals to react defensively—in the case of the electric cat, to emit an electric shock.

The shock of an electric catfish, *Malapterurus electricus,* can cause quite a reaction, although the jolt is rarely dangerous. *Photo by:* J. O'Malley.

The Catfish Aquarium

Adding Catfish to Existing Aquaria

Most catfishes kept by aquarists are added to existing community aquaria instead of having aquaria designed around them. For this approach, it is the catfish that should fit the aquarium rather than the aquarium fitting the fish. Alterations can be made in any existing aquarium setup, of course, but it is often more practical to search for a fish that blends into the existing system than to redesign an aquarium. With this approach, a number of factors should be considered. Size of the catfish must be thought of—both when it is acquired and when it is fully grown. Placing a small but rapidly growing predatory catfish in a community tank full of small barbs and tetras will necessitate a change and, probably, restocking of the tank all too quickly. The presence of plants must also be considered, for several reasons. Plants requiring long periods of high-intensity light are not compatible with the low-light preferences of many catfishes. One or the other will be placed in less-than-optimal conditions, or, worse, both may suffer. Similarly, catfishes that forage on vegetation or burrow in the substrate and uproot plants cannot be placed in planted aquaria without some amount of damage. In broader terms, the chemical environment set up for a community aquarium often reflects the environment of the targeted fishes; for example, the hard, alkaline waters of the African great lakes can easily be simulated in order to provide a suitable environment for mbuna and other African cichlids. Tanks designed for these fishes cannot be thought of as also appropriate for any of the catfishes that are routinely found in soft, acidic waters. In summary, consideration of what catfishes to add to an existing community aquarium should be based on a good understanding of what the long-term results of the addition will be for both the catfish and the rest of the community.

Some catfishes seem to be made for community aquaria and can be added to a wide variety of communities with good results. Species of the genus *Corydoras* always come to mind as community residents, and rightfully so. Most species of corys are tolerant of a wide range of aquarium conditions and are compatible with most other aquarium fishes. In addition, they are active fishes that bring life to the bottom of many community aquaria. Unfortunately, too many people who choose to add corys to their community aquaria do themselves and the corys a disservice by buying either one or a "pair" of these fishes. Corys are social, gregarious fishes that should be kept in larger groups. Kept singly, a cory may seem quite content rummaging around the bottom of the tank, but this activity is nothing compared with the bustle of a half dozen or more together along the bottom, seemingly in perpetual motion. What makes this even more attractive is that corys seem not to mind hanging out with members of different species. Thus, a collection of corys can be either of one species or of as many species as you have individuals, depending on your taste. Most of what is said here applies equally to other members of the family Callichthyidae. Only a few (relatively rare) species of *Corydoras* and adult *Hoplosternum* males in breeding condition tend to be antisocial, and even they are like that only with conspecifics. Often the decision of what species to include in a community aquarium is left to consideration of the size fish that best suits the tank.

Other catfishes lend themselves to being added to community tanks almost as well as corys. Most doradids, and especially any of the raphaels, do quite well in almost any community so long as a suitable daytime shelter is available. Like corys, raphaels will eat a wide range of prepared foods, so feeding isn't a problem. Raphaels are generally solitary animals but do not usually object to the addition of other members of the same or a related species. In fact, an exceptionally attractive hiding place may be packed with several of these catfishes while an apparently identical shelter goes empty. The same is generally true of species of *Synodontis,* although some species can be aggressive toward other mochokids, and mochokids are less likely to roam around the aquarium in the light. Loricariids are often added to community aquaria, primarily as worker fish. Because most loricariids are quite active in lighted tanks, they are quite appropriate additions to community aquaria, and probably would do better if not thought of as just workers. As discussed in the chapter "Keeping Catfishes in the Aquarium," workers all too often are left to fend for themselves without consideration of dietary needs. This seems especially true for the commonly seen *Hypostomus* species that are routinely sold under the name "plecostomus cats"

(or just "plecos"); they seem to be thought of only as workers.

A Catfish Aquarium

Designing an aquarium around a catfish, or a planned community that includes catfish, is a different matter entirely. Consideration can be given to the kinds of catfish that are of most interest, and the aquarium designed around them. In so doing, several factors must be considered: substratum, tank size and shape, water conditions, filtration, lighting, and food.

Substratum: For all but a handful of catfishes (those open-water species that spend most of their time swimming in the water column), the nature of the bottom, or substratum (or substrate), should be given prime consideration in the design of any catfish aquarium. Quite a number of catfish species spend most, if not all, of their time in close contact with the substratum, and inappropriately designed aquarium bottoms may not only make the fish uncomfortable, they could be dangerous to their health. The kinds and textures of materials used to create the substratum and the organization of these materials in space can make or break a catfish aquarium. This is not to say that an elegant design is necessarily important, or even good. In fact, a bare-bottom tank with an inverted flower pot may suffice for some species, and such a tank may be the most appropriate design.

The substratum can be thought of as consisting of three components: base, structure, and shelter. The base is particulate matter that covers part or all of the bottom of the aquarium. In general, the base is sand or gravel, but it may also be a finer silt, leaf litter, or occasionally nothing at all. The base is often the main component; it is here that most catfishes rest, feed, and search for food. The mouth, abdomen, fins, and barbels of catfish are often in contact with the base and can be affected by its nature. Bases made of sharp-edged materials, such as ground glass or coralline fragments, can readily abrade soft catfish skin. Continuous exposure to an abrasive base can wear down the skin surface and eventually expose the subdermal layers. Not only does this exposure cause pain, it opens the area to secondary bacterial and fungal infections. Even the less abrasive substrates can be harmful. Catfishes that root around for food often push their snouts into the base to extract a buried morsel. The resistance of large grains to this type of movement can cause a certain amount of wear and tear on the tissues of the snout, including their exposed barbels. Smaller-grained substrates offer less resistance to pushing around and cause less damage. The extreme case of this is seen in catfishes that actually bury themselves, exposing their entire bodies to the abrasive action of the substrate. Most catfishes that bury themselves in nature do so in very fine sand or leaf litter, not the comparatively coarse gravels so commonly used as aquarium bases.

The base also serves a role in aquarium filtration, especially when undergravel filters are used. Fine-grained bases and leaf litter bases are inappropriate for undergravel filtration and must not be used. As stated above, the substratum is the primary consideration for the catfish aquarium. If a choice needs to be made between a coarser base for undergravel filtration and a finer one, the deciding factor should be the kind of catfish and the base that would be best for it, with a filter appropriate for that substrate.

The second component of substrates is structure, the elements that provide three-dimensionality to the substratum and determine the number of catfishes that can be included in many aquaria. Just as a high-rise apartment complex can house a much larger number of people per unit area than can a single-story house, a well-designed, structurally complex substratum can provide more living spaces for catfishes than can a simple bottom. Structure also breaks up the aquarium into what fishes seem to perceive as definable subunits. These can be used as boundaries, often reducing the territory size to below what it would be in structureless aquaria. Because structure is related to the numbers of fish, aquaria destined to hold one or two fishes may not require any added structure; in fact, structure might detract from the system. Thus, the amount of structure given to an aquarium should reflect the numbers of catfishes that are to be added.

Structure can be added to aquarium substrates in a number of ways. Natural-looking aquascapes that attempt to capture the environment from which catfishes come can be structured with rockwork and driftwood. Natural-looking structure adds to both the aesthetic appeal of the tank and the complexity of the environment. Coral, which is widely used in marine aquaria to add structure, is inappropriate in most freshwater systems and is definitely not desirable in catfish aquaria. The extremely sharp edges of the coral skeleton are hazardous to catfish skin, and the calcium carbonate matrix of coral adds unwanted alkalinity and hardness to the water.

Structure need not attempt to recre-

Angular rocks piled on top of one another provide both structure and shelter for catfishes. *Photo by:* W. Staeck.

ate a natural look. Simplified substitutes can be used to add three-dimensionality to an aquarium without its resembling an actual aquatic environment. The results are fully functional and offer the added advantage of making the aquarium more easily converted as the demands on it change. Readily available substitutes include PVC piping, clay pots (including broken ones), and such commercially available products as Lok-Rocks™ and partially hollowed-out ceramic blocks. The choice, size, and amount of these structures to be included depend on the size and number of fishes in the aquarium. Often experimentation is needed to produce the correct amount and spacing of structures, but this becomes easier with practice.

Structure is closely related to the third category of substrata: shelter. Shelter can be defined as spaces that accommodate resting or hiding fishes. The absence of structure in the substratum greatly limits the possibilities of shelter for catfishes. Burrowing catfishes, such as banjo catfishes, find shelter in the base of the substrate, and, to a limited degree, plants offer shelter to some catfishes. But real shelter for catfishes generally comes from appropriately designed structures. That is not to say that a large amount of structure necessarily offers an abundance of shelter. Highly structured aquaria may be very attractive but still short on appropriate shelters.

Catfish are often at home in shelters that seem to be too small for them. Large, open spaces offer little shelter to catfishes and are usually ignored by them. Instead, improbably small openings in rockwork or tubular structures that seem impenetrably small are usually preferred. An abundance of shelters offers a choice to aquarium inhabitants, something that is often necessary, especially for subordinate members of a pecking order. Varying the size, shape, and direction of openings adds to the choices that the fishes have in selecting a shelter that is most suitable.

Shelters afford protection in a variety of ways. Many catfishes are nocturnal and seek shelter from daylight and aquarium lights, either in completely enclosed areas or in shadow. For this, overhanging rockwork or floating plants often are sufficient. If designed correctly, a shelter from light can be positioned so that the fish is readily seen and yet is completely at home, giving the aquarist the best of both worlds. Most *Synodontis* catfishes seem particularly sensitive to light and need only a shelter of this type to be content. Other catfishes seem to need more from shelters. Most doradids, auchenipterids, and centromochlids, for example, seem to prefer shelters that keep them in the dark *and* provide a certain amount of confined space. They select shelters that are so small they can barely wedge themselves in, and from which they cannot readily be pried out.

The need for adequate shelters is most acute in aquaria that are intended for spawning of catfishes. The male of a spawning pair often becomes extremely protective of the newly produced egg mass and will relentlessly chase tankmates away from the vicinity. Providing several shelters will help the female avoid the wrath of the protective male.

It should be mentioned here that the need for catfish to find an adequate shelter can cause at least one important health problem that can and should be avoided by a forward-looking aquarist. One apparently appealing place for many catfishes to find shelter is the tiny crevice between most aquarium heaters and the walls of the aquarium. Almost invariably, one (or more) catfish will try to wedge itself in this crevice. So long as the heater is off, the space serves as an adequate shelter; however, the glass surface of the functioning heater gets very hot and can seriously burn the catfish. At very little cost, a plastic mesh cylinder can be purchased that surrounds the glass heater tube, providing a fraction of an inch of space between the heater glass and the fish—enough to prevent the skin from being burned. This type of protection should be in place in any catfish aquarium.

Tank Size and Shape: The generally used measure for the number of fishes that can be accommodated in an aquarium is the size, and especially the volume, of the aquarium. This is most valuable for free-swimming fishes, which roam around the entire aquarium. Most catfishes, however, tend to use only the bottom of the aquarium, and the volume of the aquarium is largely wasted. A better measure of the number of catfish to be included in an aquarium is the surface area of the bottom, or the structured bottom (see page 53 for a discussion of structure). In other words, two aquaria of the same volume can accommodate different numbers of catfish, depending on the tank's surface area and the structure that is added to it.

The "correct" size and shape of a catfish aquarium depends to a large degree on the goals the keeper has for a particular fish. A tank destined to hold a catfish that you keep as a pet may be comparatively small and chosen to provide maximum viewing of the fish. The same species if kept for breeding would probably best be kept in a proportionally larger tank. But the concept of correct size is a vague one and may not be important by itself. It is important to provide a tank that is large enough for the fish to swim around and turn around in, but that isn't always possible (especially with rather long, slender catfishes). A number of healthy, well-maintained catfishes are in aquaria that are not large enough to allow them to turn around without great effort.

The factor that makes aquarium size of interest is generally the amount of water in the aquarium. Tanks with larger amounts of water have a natural buffering ability, thereby minimizing the impact of any change on the resident fishes. Changes in external temperature and in water chemistry and quality can adversely affect fishes, especially if they occur quickly. Because of this, large aquaria have a distinct

Many banjo catfish, such as this craggy-headed banjo (*Bunocephalus scabriceps*), are at home in a sand or leaf litter substratum. *Photo by:* C. Ferraris.

advantage over smaller ones.

Unfortunately, there are several equally important disadvantages to large aquaria, such as weight, cost, and space. More often than not, the decision on the size of an aquarium is based on these criteria and not on the fish it will hold. This being the case, it should be realized that the choice of catfish should reflect the realities of your aquarium. If the aquarium is overstocked, with either too many fish or too large a fish, it is doubly important that other factors such as water conditions and aquarium structure be monitored to provide a minimum of stress on the fishes.

Water Conditions: It should be no surprise that the conditions of the aquarium water are of major importance to a healthy catfish aquarium. No fish can be expected to be happy in water resembling that found in a sewer, and yet all too often that is exactly the case in aquaria.

Factors of the condition of water as they affect aquarium fishes can be di-

vided into two major categories: those independent of the fact that the water is part of an aquarium and those directly related to the aquarium conditions. Independent factors are usually termed "water chemistry" by aquarists, and include the hardness, pH, salinity, and heavy metal concentrations of the water. All natural water possesses these characteristics, and usually the water supply from a certain region (or particular well) has a more or less uniform set of chemical characteristics. Thus, water is often talked about as being hard and alkaline, or soft and acidic, in reference to the hardness and pH components. It is generally thought to be desirable to match the aquarium conditions to the chemical environment in which a fish grew up. Far too often, however, the natural conditions from which the fishes were taken are unknown or poorly known. Even when the conditions are known for a particular fish, replicating them may not be accomplished easily. It is comparatively easy to harden soft water by adding carbonates, such as crushed coral or shells, to the filtration system, but the reverse is sometimes exceptionally difficult and rarely worth the effort. Fortunately, most catfishes seem to be quite tolerant of a wide range of chemical conditions, and the efforts undertaken to create the native chemical environment may be unnecessary or of only minor importance when compared to other aquarium maintenance activities. One exception to this is the presence of large amounts of heavy metals in the water. Metal ions such as those of copper or lead can be particularly dangerous to fishes and should not be introduced into aquaria. Most often, natural water supplies do not contain dangerous concentrations of

metals, but some (especially old) plumbing systems may allow these ions into the water. The recent introduction of Polyfilter™ into the aquarium hobby seems to be a simple solution to heavy metal problems in aquarium water. Polyfilter removes these ions from the water (when placed directly in an aquarium or in a power filter system) by fixing the ions on the filter pad, which is thrown away when saturated.

With the exception of heavy metals, the actual chemical composition of the water in which most fish are placed is far less important than is the speed with which fish are transferred from one set of water conditions to another. The shock of a quick transfer involving even comparatively minor changes in pH may be more harmful to a fish than a drastic change done over several hours. A simple but effective method of introducing a fish to a new chemical environment is called "dripping over" a fish, or the "drip method." A fish to be introduced into a new chemical environment is placed in a container of its own water (that is, the water it has been living in or transported in). New water is siphoned from an aquarium or aquarium system into the container holding the fish. The speed of this transfer, which is all-important, should be very slow, to the point where water drips, one drop at a time, through the siphon (hence the name "drip method"). At least ten times the volume of the original water container should be allowed to drip through the system, after which the water that surrounds the fish will be almost identical to the targeted water supply. The total time for this process should depend to a great degree on the difference in chemistry of the two waters. If the pH difference of the water is 1 or less, an hour should be sufficient. Larger gradients in pH demand proportionally longer periods of dripping. During this transfer process, the fish should be allowed to remain as calm as possible. An agitated fish passes much more water across its gills than does a calm one, and the quick change in water chemistry will have a greater effect on the fish's delicate gill membranes. Because of this, it is usually better to transfer a fish in a quiet corner or overnight, when there is likely to be the least amount of traffic around the aquaria.

The water chemistry of an established aquarium should not change with time unless that is the intention. Changes in pH can result from poor nitrogen cycling (see below), which can be caused by either poor aquarium management or overcrowding of fish. Sometimes overcrowding is a necessary evil when keeping large fishes. It is almost impossible to provide a large pet catfish with a volume of water equivalent to what is normally given fishes in a spawning aquarium or even a community tank. Because of this, pet fish will add comparatively large amounts of wastes to their tank's water. These wastes tend to change the nitrogen content of the water and thereby the pH.

When water chemistry changes occur, action must be taken to stop or at least buffer them. Soft water seems to be most vulnerable to rapid changes in pH. Increased water hardness has a buffering effect on this type of waste-induced pH change.

Nitrogenous compounds in the water are the direct result of the digestive activities of the fishes and bacteria in all aquaria. The accumulation of nitrogenous compounds in aquaria is generally referred to by aquarists as the quality of the water, or water quality. The water quality can greatly affect the health and activity of fishes and is of far greater concern than most of the water chemistry parameters mentioned earlier.

Aquarium water is constantly being inundated with food left uneaten, as well as waste products excreted or defecated by the fishes. These additions to the water are converted by both chemical reactions and bacterial action into soluble nitrogen-based compounds that mix with the water. These compounds undergo a predictable series of changes, called the nitrogen cycle. Bacterial action trans-

The management of nitrogenous compound cycling is one of the most important aspects of aquarium maintenance. *Illustration by:* K. Tscheschner.

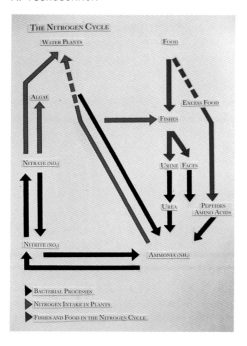

forms the undigested food and excreted wastes into ammonia, which is then changed into nitrites. Nitrites are further converted into nitrates, which in natural conditions are readily removed from the water by aquatic plants. This cycle can also be thought of as a change from relatively toxic substances to less toxic compounds. The cycling of these compounds in fully established aquaria is quite prompt, and dangerous levels of ammonia or nitrites do not normally accumulate. In newly established aquaria, however, the bacterial community has not had time to build up sufficiently to convert these two compounds quickly, and dangerous levels of one or both may accumulate. It is for this reason that in newly established aquaria the levels of all nitrogenous compounds must be monitored, and, to be on the safe side, only a minimum of fish should be added. Unfortunately, it is possible for the nitrogen cycle of an aquarium to break down, allowing an unhealthy accumulation of ammonia and nitrites to go unconverted. Such a breakdown can result from the loss of a biological filter, mechanical malfunction of the pumping system, or poisoning of the bacteria responsible for the nitrogen conversions, possibly through the use of antibiotics in an aquarium. One of the most common ways in which the nitrogen cycle is disrupted is by the well-meaning efforts of comparatively new aquarists who try too hard to keep an aquarium clean. Changing the water and filter media is important to the regular maintenance of any aquarium, but the water and filter harbor nitrogen-fixing bacteria that are essential to the nitrogen cycle. If a major water change is done to an aquarium at the same time the filter is cleaned, a substantial portion of the bacterial colony is removed from the aquarium all at once. The remaining bacteria may be too few to handle the task before them. It should be an unbroken rule, therefore, that the filter and the water are never changed at the same time if any fish are in the aquarium.

A breakdown of nitrogen cycling can be hazardous to fishes and therefore should be checked for regularly. The breakdown of nitrogen cycling usually causes simultaneous increases in ammonia and nitrites and changes in pH. Together, these changes can be thought of as causing chemical or environmental stress to the fishes.

In catfishes, environmental stress is usually first detected in the barbels around the mouth. Especially in long-barbeled, naked catfishes, the barbels dramatically deteriorate in water that is not cycling nitrogen properly. Starting from the tip, the barbels seem to lose their rigidity and dangle at awkward angles relative to the base of the barbel, and eventually drop off. As time goes on, a greater portion of the barbel is affected, until nothing is left of it except a thread of mucus. The combination of ever-shortening barbels and the loss of rigidity of the portion that remains are sure signs of a problem with the water. In catfishes with shorter barbels, such as corys and whips, the barbel damage is still a real problem, but much less obvious to the casual observer. A close look will often reveal that the barbels of corys kept in community aquaria that are not well maintained are little more than stumps.

A second and more serious problem that sometimes arises is the formation of round or oval wounds on the skin of the belly, chin, and lips of catfishes. *Chaca* seems particularly likely to exhibit this condition, and most deaths of these fishes are correlated with these wounds. As with barbel degeneration, this seems to be directly caused by water conditions.

Filtration: As in all aquarium systems, filtration is essential for the proper maintenance of healthy catfish aquaria. Filtration systems provide a variety of services for the aquarium. In any of several ways, particulate matter is trapped and removed from the water, which makes the water clearer. Filtration systems also move water over an established bacterial population that converts the ammonia and nitrites into comparatively harmless nitrates. Certain classes of soluble compounds other than nitrogenous wastes can be removed to some extent by ion-exchange filters.

No one filter or filtration system can do all types of filtration well. Thus, the appropriate system for an aquarium depends on the anticipated filtration problems. For example, pet catfishes are usually kept in comparatively small tanks of water. The amount of nitrogenous waste that accumulates in a tank of this type is quite large, and the filtration system must have the potential to accommodate this influx of ammonia. Unless a large biological filtration system is in place, the ammonia and nitrite concentrations can soon build up to lethal levels. Aquaria designed to keep loricariids, especially larger species, will have a tremendous amount of particulate waste, due to the large amounts of undigested food that pass through their guts and the wood fragments that are scraped from the necessary driftwood in the aquarium. Without mechanical filters an aquarium of this type would be continually clouded.

To say that one type of filter or another is of prime importance does not mean that another is unnecessary. In fact, a combination of mechanical and biological filtration is always needed. Only the relative contributions of each may vary.

A variety of filter designs can serve each of these filtration functions. A good introductory book on aquarium design and maintenance can provide you with all the possibilities. It is important to consult a recently published book for this, because filtration technology is changing rapidly, and many currently available options will not be found in books even a few years old. When deciding on a filter system, keep in mind that although different systems can do essentially the same job, the filter may affect the catfish residents quite markedly. For example, undergravel filters are generally quite good biological filters but are not the best design for catfishes that burrow. Burrowers require fine substrates that, by their very nature, are unsuitable for undergravel filtration.

Lighting: Correct lighting for a catfish aquarium is in many ways different from that for just about any other kind of freshwater aquarium fish. Bright lights are just about the worst way to treat most catfishes, and catfishes kept under such conditions usually repay their keepers by residing in the most secluded part of the aquarium. Many catfish would be quite content in an aquarium without lights, with only ambient room light to break up the total darkness. While this may be more satisfactory to the fishes, it certainly leaves a bit to be desired by anyone wanting to observe the catfish! Thus, a compromise between these two extremes must be made.

There are at least two distinct possibilities for illuminating an aquarium in the best interests of both the catfish and their keepers. The first and most commonly employed is to provide the aquarium with subdued lighting. Reducing the amount of light that enters the aquarium can be accomplished in a number of ways. If the primary source of light is incandescent bulbs, using lower wattage bulbs may be sufficient. If it isn't, or if the primary light source is from fluorescent tubes, you may need to filter the light. A piece of translucent white plastic placed between the light source and the aquarium glass will substantially reduce the amount of light reaching the aquarium. In community aquaria it may not be feasible or desirable to reduce the light entering the aquarium, especially if living plants are desired. In this case it may be necessary to shade part of the aquarium with part of the internal structure. Overhanging ledges may shade enough of the tank bottom to accommodate at least some of the catfishes. Large, broad-leafed aquatic plants such as Amazon swords can reduce the amount of light that reaches the aquarium substrate, especially when they are planted in clusters. Similarly, thick mats of floating plants may keep at least part of the aquarium bottom well shaded. I'm sure there are numerous other ways of providing at least partial shade in a community aquarium.

Reducing the amount of white light entering the aquarium will make almost all catfishes, even the day-active species (corys, plecos, and their relatives), more comfortable. There are, however, quite a number of catfishes that will not be coaxed out of hiding in any amount of light. If you wish to watch these species, you may want to use red light to illuminate the aquarium. In an otherwise darkened room, red light provides enough light for most people to see the aquarium quite well, even though the fish are apparently unable to detect the light, acting as they would in total or near total darkness. Catfish that seem to do nothing besides rest on the aquarium bottom can be seen gliding along the length of the tank, sometimes with a gracefulness that is totally unexpected.

Setting up an aquarium or aquarium room for red-light viewing is quite straightforward. Red incandescent lights can be purchased at hardware stores or, failing that, a good photographic supply store. Fluorescent fixtures can be covered with red cellophane to filter the light; tape the edges of the cellophane to the light fixture with an opaque tape (such as black electrician's tape), so that no white light escapes. Remember, red-light catfish watching is effective only in an otherwise dark room. Using a red light on an aquarium in a sunny room will do nothing to induce catfishes to come out of hiding.

Food: No discussion of catfish keeping would be complete without mention of the nutritional requirements of these fishes. Fortunately, feeding catfishes is one of the easiest parts of their maintenance, as most catfishes are quite tolerant of a wide variety of foods. Most of the catfishes that are available in the hobby can be successfully raised on any of the good-quality commercially prepared foods (flakes, pellets, and so forth), although there are some notable exceptions.

One thing that catfishes cannot survive is complete neglect. The notion that catfishes are scavengers or "mud suckers" and can make due with little or no attention is a long-standing misconception that must be forgotten to successfully keep catfish.

Feeding catfishes involves two activities: selecting an appropriate food and getting it to the catfish. A great many catfishes tend to be opportunistic feeders and eat a wide variety of foods. This is good news for most catfish keepers, as it means that catfish are usually not as finicky as their four-legged namesakes. They readily accept almost any living, frozen, or dried food offered to them, provided they can somehow fit it into their mouths. In addition, the great majority of catfishes seen in the aquarium hobby can be trained to eat prepared foods. These come in a variety of forms, but they can be thought of as belonging to two major types: flakes and pellets.

Flakes are thin sheets of food that readily crumble into small wafers. In water the wafers readily break up into even smaller bits. This makes flakes unsuitable for any but the smallest catfishes or those that tend to stay at or near the surface, such as glass cats and debauwi cats. Catfish mouths and stomachs are large and able to consume large volumes of food. Only corys and a few other catfishes are really well equipped to handle the small particles of food that result from the gently sinking flakes.

Pellets, on the other hand, are quite well suited to the feeding habits of most catfishes. Pellets are formed by compressing the prepared food into uniform-sized blocks (usually in the form of a small cylinder). Depending on the amount of air that is trapped in the food during the processing, the pellet either sinks or floats in the water. Because most catfishes are more at home near the bottom of the aquarium, sinking pellets are most often the appropriate choice. Tetra has at least two kinds of sinking pel-

lets that are quite appropriate for catfishes: Tetra Bits® and DoroMarin®. There are times when floating pellets can or should be used in catfish aquaria. Midwater catfishes, such as the glass catfish and debauwi cats and almost all members of the families Auchenipteridae and Centromochlidae, are quite at home feeding from the surface of the water on floating pellets. Some *Synodontis* and even a few armored suckermouth cats will take food from the surface, at least on occasion. Thus, it is not inappropriate to have both sinking and floating pellets available and to experiment with both on newly acquired catfishes.

Unlike most catfishes, armored suckermouth catfishes (plecos, whiptails, blue eyes, snow kings, and so on) are all vegetarians. Their diet needs to contain a high proportion of plant matter, which can come from algae growing in the tank, vegetable matter, or high-vegetable food pellets.

A single aquarium cannot produce sufficient algae to maintain plecos in healthy condition for very long. Plecos eat a tremendous amount for their size and will quickly clean out an algae-filled tank. Aquarists who employ worker catfishes to clean excess algae from the glass of a tank often end up moving these fishes from one aquarium to another to keep them from running out of food. So long as the individual aquaria are kept reasonably similar in environment, the transfer from tank to tank can be made with little stress to the catfish. If you don't have several algae-filled tanks, however, this system is doomed to failure. Large plecos (and some species get very large indeed) cannot easily be maintained this way, for a variety of reasons, most important of which is the inherent difficulty of moving large

Leoparacanthicus galaxias is one of several species of very attractive armored suckermouth catfishes that have only recently been discovered. *Photo by:* R. Stawikowski.

and surprisingly strong fish from tank to tank against their will. For this reason alone, it is better to bring food to these large fishes than bring the fishes to the food. In wide use now is green summer squash, or zucchini, as the primary or only food for many plecos. Preparing squash for feeding is quite simple. In the extreme, just slice it up into rounds ½ inch to 1 inch thick, weight the pieces down, and throw them into the tank. Raw squash will float, which explains why it needs to be weighted. Alternatively, the squash can be parboiled, which makes it dense enough to sink. Cooking can be accomplished in a pan of boiling water or a microwave oven. Cooking tends to diminish the nutritive value of the squash, however, especially destroying the vitamins. Cooking should therefore be kept to an absolute minimum: just enough to cause the slices to sink gently to the bottom of the aquarium. The squash rings will be eaten from the inside out, with only a few seeds remaining after a couple of days. Probably any of the summer squashes—for example, crookneck and scalloped—would serve equally well.

If feeding catfish squash sounds too good to be true, it is—but only a little too good. The one problem that has to be overcome is getting the catfish started on this altogether foreign food. A large disk-shaped object, which may be as large as the fish itself, descending through the water cannot appear too tempting a meal for any fish, and may more likely frighten away a fish than attract it. The key is allowing fish to get used to the new food without starving to death meanwhile; so intro-

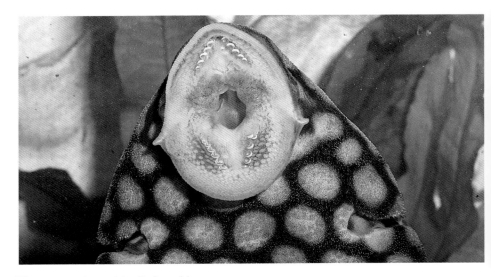

The spoon-shaped teeth found in all members of the genus *Panaque* allow these fishes to rasp large quantities of wood. *Photo by:* P. Loiselle.

duce it along with other foods. In the case of plecos, it is best to introduce squash into a tank with some algae and let the fish explore the strange new object in the tank. Squash will soon be readily taken and algae all but forgotten!

Some but not all armored sucker-mouth cats seem to be quite content eating high-vegetable-content pelletized foods. An important thing to keep in mind with commercially prepared products is that the food, whether flakes for small fish or pellets for larger ones, must be high in vegetable matter and contain vitamins (especially vitamin C).

Finally, in all tanks that contain plecos there should be some driftwood. Most of these catfishes spend a great deal of their time on the wood and scrape at its surface. Some if not

all loricariids may require wood in their diet, and will scrape at anything that even remotely resembles wood in an attempt to fulfill this need. There is strong evidence that at least some pleco relatives obtain nutrition from the wood. Without driftwood, you may be depriving your fish of an essential source of food and at the same time inviting an unnecessary potential problem. Wood-scraping plecos (most noteworthy of this group are the panaques) have sufficiently strong teeth and jaws to scrape easily through many plastics. In the absence of wood, plastics such as the lift tubes of power filters may be attacked and destroyed. Another and certainly worse problem can occur if the silicone sealer around the edge of an aquarium is the only scrapable substance in the aquarium. More than one aquarist has had to repair or discard a large tank that was victimized by a pleco (and I'm not even mentioning the mess that invariably results from a tank that springs a leak). Along the same line, it is worth noting that plexiglass aquaria are *not* suitable for any plecos. Unlike glass, plexiglass succumbs to scraping. Although it is unlikely that any but the largest panaques could actually completely penetrate the walls of a plexiglass aquarium, their efforts will quickly result in an unsightly scratched surface, through which it is all but impossible to see.

Making sure that the food intended for catfishes actually gets to them is not always easy. Many catfishes are nocturnal and will not venture out into a lighted aquarium even for food. This can be a special problem in community aquaria, in which more active tankmates may well consume all the available food long before the catfishes ever have a chance. While some nocturnal catfish can be trained to feed in the light, others seem unable or unwilling to learn. In such cases it is necessary to provide food just before the aquarium is darkened, to maximize the chance that the retiring catfishes can get food.

Problems

Catfishes, like all other aquarium-kept fishes, are subjected to a variety of conditions and diseases that may threaten their health. In many cases the problems and treatments are pretty much universal for all freshwater fishes and need not be repeated here. A good reference book on the recognition and treatment of fish diseases is indispensable for the serious fish keeper and can be referred to for problems encountered with your catfishes that are not covered in this chapter. There are a few conditions that are either special to catfishes or more commonly encountered in these fishes and thus deserve mention here.

Problems resulting from water qual-

Most species of *Corydoras*, such as this *C. schwartzi*, are quite hardy and can tolerate a large range of aquarium conditions. However, they cannot tolerate too high a buildup of nitrogenous wastes. *Photo by:* J. O'Malley.

ity changes in the aquarium have already been discussed. Drastic changes in pH or the nitrogen balance can have marked effects on catfishes. Curiously, the otherwise hardy *Corydoras* catfishes are among the most susceptible to nitrogenous waste buildup. In community aquaria, corys are often the first to succumb, and should be considered an early warning of a greater number of casualties if immediate action is not taken to correct the situation.

The all-too-common aquarium fish parasite known as "ick" is a special problem for catfish keepers. Ick itself is bad enough for catfishes, but the generally used treatment for most other aquarium fishes is even worse. Most ick remedies involve chemicals that are irritants to catfishes. They also require elevated water temperatures to stimulate a transformation of the parasite into its free-swimming and most vulnerable phase. This added heat in the tank is one of the worst things that can be done to a stressed catfish, so the "cure" can often be fatal.

Thus, an alternative approach to ick treatment is warranted. Ick usually shows up later on catfishes than on many other fishes. In a community aquarium the catfish may seem unaffected when other fishes are severely infected. In cases such as this, remove catfishes from the community tank that needs to be treated for ick. Allow the treatment to proceed and simultaneously observe the catfishes to be sure they do not develop signs of ick. When the remaining fish are cured and the tank temperature is back to normal, reintroduce the catfishes. If the catfishes show any sign of disease, do not return them to the community tank, thereby reinfecting the

tank. If it is not possible to separate the catfishes from the infected fishes, or if the catfishes are themselves infected, it is necessary to use another approach. Some ick remedies, such as Jungle's Ick Guard II, are designed for catfishes and other fishes vulnerable to traditional ick cures. These formalin-based products are less toxic to catfishes and do not require elevated water temperatures. This comparatively new approach to ick treatment seems to work equally well on all fishes and thus may be a better all-around treatment for ick. When using one of these products, it is very important to (1) do a partial water change before beginning the treatment; (2) remove all carbon-based filtration systems for the treatment period; and (3) adhere to the dosage and follow-up treatment instructions on the label.

Unlike much of the aquarium fish hobby, a large proportion of catfishes are still collected from the wild. They are more likely to bring with them parasites that are not often a problem with pond- or tank-reared fishes. It is not uncommon to find that these fishes harbor gill or digestive tract crustacean or worm parasites. In the weakened state that normally results from the long international transport, these fishes may have a thriving parasitic infection that further weakens the fish. With luck and a bit of tender loving care by their keepers, the catfishes can often repel this infection without any other assistance. This TLC should be the first course of action. Attempts at eliminating the parasite by chemical means should be used only as a last resort.

One specific type of parasite problem and treatment should be mentioned here: smooth-skinned catfish seem to be susceptible to intestinal worm parasites. A good indication of the problem is found when a fish has a healthy appetite but does not seem to grow. Occasionally this can be noticed in a single fish, but it is much more obvious when several of the same species are acquired at the same time (and at approximately the same initial size) and kept together. If one seems to grow at a substantially slower rate, worms may well be the cause. I have seen successful purging of worms with Piperazine citrate. As with any chemical, this product should be used only as a last resort. Curing the problem may well have disastrous side effects.

A problem that is not caused by parasites or other disease organisms but must be mentioned here is an affliction of armored suckermouth catfish called "hollow belly." With the exception of a few species currently being pond-bred in Florida, most species of loricariids are imported from the wild. Although reasonably hardy fishes, they often make their entrance into the aquarium market in a very weakened state and in need of immediate care. Unlike the great majority of catfishes, loricariids, being herbivores, require food often and in large quantities. The total time that these fishes are kept without food—including the time they are held in South America, packed for export and actually shipped, held at the importer and wholesaler's tanks, and finally at the retailer before being sold to the customer—far exceeds the catfishes' ability to fast comfortably. The result of this overlong starvation is the onset of emaciation. The hard dermal scutes covering the body of these fishes obscure the emaciated condition of the fish, and the true condition can be told only by looking at parts of the catfish

body not covered by this armor. Any moderately starved loricariid will exhibit the justly named hollow belly, in which the comparatively flexible underbelly of many species in this family (but not most whiptails, which have large belly scutes) becomes concave. This is especially noticeable when a fish is taken from the water and held upside down. The skin on the belly collapses into the abdominal cavity and looks quite hollow. In contrast, well-fed catfishes will have a rounded or at least flat belly. Logically, fish with hollow belly are in need of food, and lots of it. An algae-laden aquarium is probably the best place to start a fish in this condition. In the absence of a suitable aquarium, any source of vegetable matter will suffice. The key is to get the fish eating something as soon as possible. The longer a loricariid languishes in an aquarium without eating, the less likely it is ever to eat.

Hollow belly is the first and least serious symptom of starvation in suckermouth catfish. A more seriously starved loricariid can be recognized by its sunken eyes. Unlike hollow belly, sunken eyes can be seen readily in all members of the family, including the whiptails. In healthy loricariids the eyeball projects beyond the margin of the bony rim (called the orbit) of the eye. In a severely starved catfish the eye will slowly recede toward the middle of the head and will be pulled away from the orbit, so that it does not project out beyond the rim. By the time sunken eyes are readily apparent, the fish has been without food for too long, and its chance of survival is very small. A fish in this condition will also have a very bad case of hollow belly, and the fish is quite likely to show the seriousness of its condition by the near absence of movement, except when chased. Un-

A doradid catfish, *Acanthodoras cataphractus,* emitting fluid from its pectoral gland. *Photo by:* C. Ferraris.

fortunately, fish with sunken eyes will often not eat, making recovery nearly impossible. Thus, it is rarely a good gamble to acquire a fish that has sunken eyes. Only an extremely rare loricariid, offered at an exceptionally good price, should be considered. Even then, an old adage applies here: Any deal that seems too good to be true probably is!

Catfish injuries are often the result of placing incompatible fishes together in an aquarium. This is more correctly a human problem than a catfish one and is caused by the general condition of too many interesting catfishes and too few places to put them. Many armored suckermouth catfishes, bagrids, and species of the genus *Synodontis* do not readily tolerate other members of their own or closely related species. If adequate tank space (or defined spaces, as described in "Substratum," above) is unavailable, the catfishes will vie for their share of the space. Invariably one catfish will win out, at the expense of the other(s). Thus, it rarely serves any useful purpose to add additional *Synodontis* or loricariids to an aquarium that already has a stable number. The most likely outcome is that the number of healthy fish will stay the same and the added ones will only be vanquished and in need of serious attention.

Keepers of doradid catfishes may notice a peculiar milky-white fluid oozing out of the sides of an otherwise healthy-looking fish. This is especially noticeable when an individual is removed from an aquarium, but it can be seen in some catfishes swimming freely in the water. The fluid comes from a gland at the base of the pectoral fin called the pectoral gland. The function of the gland is unknown and in need of study. There is no indication that the fluid is irritating to undamaged skin, so handling a fish that is releasing fluid need not be avoided. It is possible that a newly opened cut may be sensitive enough that the fluid could cause a burning sensation. In the water, usually only small amounts are released, and they are quickly removed from the water by most filtration systems. Although at first glance this substance may appear to indicate a problem, it is instead an indication of a healthy, active doradid catfish showing off one more mystery to be solved by future catfish researchers.

Finally, one recently discovered catfish "problem" that has come to light in recent issues of a few aquarium magazines needs to be mentioned: now that aquarists are keeping banjo catfish in separate aquaria, they have discovered that these fishes will occasionally lose the surface of their skin in large chunks (see the Aspredinidae family account for more details). It has been suggested that this behavior may be the result of high bacteria populations in the substrate or a dangerously low pH of the water. This seems not to be the case at all. Perfectly healthy banjo catfishes shed their skin at more or less regular intervals. The shedding seems to be similar to that of snakes and lizards, and *not* an indication of a problem. Most catfishes do not shed skin, but banjos, including the long-tailed species, and the Asian catfish family Akysidae (which I call "Asian banjos," because of their similarity in appearance to the South American species) all undergo skin shedding. Thus, shed skin in these fishes should not be cause for concern.

The milky fluid released by doradid catfish may be irritating if it is allowed to enter an open wound. *Photo by:* C. Ferraris.

Reproduction

Telling the Boys from the Girls

The great diversity of forms found in catfishes is reflected in the great variation found in the patterns of sexual dimorphism. In some species members of one sex are so similar to the other that it's a wonder they can tell each other apart. At the other extreme, it is sometimes hard to believe that males and females belong to the same species. Of course, most catfishes fall somewhere in between, and with a little experience they can be sexed with some degree of confidence.

Sexual differences fall into two categories: those that appear at the onset of adulthood and persist throughout life and those exhibited only when the individual is at peak reproductive con-

dition, disappearing at other times. The distinction between these two can be extremely important when trying to determine whether the fishes that you are about to obtain are really a pair. At this time we are still in the process of discovering sexual differences in many species, and the question of permanency of these features has not been addressed.

In most if not all catfishes, at least two external features can be used to help distinguish males from females. Healthy adult females are more robust than males, and, provided you have at least one of each sex, the differences are often quite obvious. Hours or even a day after last having eaten, females often can look as if they were just fed. This is especially obvious when the female is heavily laden with mature eggs, but the difference in girth sometimes can be detected year round. In addition, a genital papilla, found at the base of the anal fin, is often obviously

A male black lancer clearly showing the extended genital papilla. *Photo by:* C. Ferraris.

A female black lancer lacking genital papilla (compare with condition in male). *Photo by:* C. Ferraris.

different between sexes. These papillae form the opening through which either eggs or sperm pass out of the body. The shape and size of this structure vary, and recognizable differences are used widely in sex determination. In some species, such as the black lancers (*Bagrichthys macropterus* and *B. macracanthus*), the harlequin lancer (*Bagroides melapterus*), and the Asian bumblebee cats (*Leiocassis* spp.), the genital papilla on the male is quite prominent and readily recognized. Unfortunately, the differences between male and female genital papillae are not always so distinctive, and this characteristic can be used only by someone experienced in sexing that species. Thus, it is of limited value for someone just beginning to work with a species.

The great majority of catfishes seem to be externally sexually dimorphic only in the two characteristics mentioned above. This is the case for all of the smooth-skinned catfishes except for the families Auchenipteridae and Centromochlidae, as well as many of the armored species. The large South American family Loricariidae is the best example of a group in which sexual dimorphism is often very pronounced. The well-known genus *Ancistrus* is perhaps the best-known example of this dimorphism, due to the prominent ornamentation on the snouts, especially in adult males. Although members of this genus are usually referred to as "bristle noses" because of their snout ornamentation, these projections are anything but bristly. Instead, the spikes are quite soft, fleshy tentacles that collapse when the fish is removed from its buoyant aquatic environment. Contrary to widespread belief, both males and females may have these bristles. In species in which this is true, the bristles are much more pronounced in

An adult pair of *Ancistrus* showing the sexual dimorphism in head tentacle development. The male is on the left. *Photo by:* A. van den Nieuwenhuizen.

males and are found both on the upper portion of the snout and along the anterior margin, where they occur in females. Truly stiff bristles, resembling those of toothbrushes, are found in loricariids and in fact are quite often sexually dimorphic structures. These bristles, or odontodes, are virtually identical to teeth found in the jaws of these fishes. Odontodes are placed on various parts of the body and are generally larger or more numerous in males than in females. Placement of odontodes is highly species-specific and is widely used by ichthyologists in the identification of species and the forming of genera and subfamilies. In contrast, there is little indication of how the catfish themselves use these structures. They may serve to assist in

recognition of members of the species and possibly their reproductive condition. It has been suggested that enlarged odontodes associated with the opercular region are used as weapons by males to defend their territories against other males.

As with the teeth of loricariids, odontodes fall off and are replaced periodically. At the onset of the reproductive season, odontodes of males are often replaced with exceptionally large ones, further exaggerating the dimorphism between the sexes and making it much easier to recognize adult males.

Some callichthyids also show sexual dimorphism of odontodes. In *Callichthys* and *Hoplosternum*, odontodes that are embedded in the male's pectoral spine enlarge, giving the spine a thickened appearance. These thick spines are the most obvious way of recognizing males in the reproductive state. Most *Corydoras, Brochis,* and *Aspidoras* show no indication of increased growth of odontodes and in general do not have any obvious dimorphism except for the increased girth of females. *Corydoras barbatus* and *C. macropterus,* however, are exceptional. Males grow a "Velcro mustache" along the sides of the snout, consisting of a dense patch of short odontodes. In addition, the males of both species show pronounced elongation of their pectoral fin spines, and the spines are often curved upward.

Of the smooth-skinned catfishes, the auchenipterids show the most obvious dimorphic structures. Auchenipterids are the only catfishes that undergo internal fertilization, and they have a modification of the genital papillae for this purpose. The male's papilla becomes elongate and is firmly attached to the anterior margin of the anal fin. At the tip of the elongate papilla is the genital pore, through which the sperm leave the body. The fin rays at the front of the anal fin are both enlarged and stiffened, making a rodlike gonopodium, or intromittent organ. This gonopodium gives the leading edge of the anal fin a pointed appearance instead of the gently curved margin that is seen in females and juveniles.

Many auchenipterid males also undergo a remarkable change in the size and shape of the dorsal fin spine at the beginning of the reproductive season. The spine can more than double in length and become curved into an S shape. This growth is often accompanied by the addition of a peculiar row of small spines that anchor at the front of the dorsal fin spine and curve left and right so that they point sideways or even backward. These changes in the spine all seem to permit the male to firmly grasp the female during copulation, as explained in more detail below. A few species of auchenipterids go one step further and develop elongated, stiffened maxillary barbels, which add to the strength of the male's grasp of the female.

As if that weren't enough, males of at least one species of wood cat, *Entomacorus gameroi* from Venezuela, show changes in both the pectoral fin spine and the pelvic fin, in addition to the changes described above. The spine of the pectoral fin becomes enlarged and contorted, and the first ray of the pelvic fin is changed into an elongate paddle. No one has reported on spawning activities in this species, so the function of these structures is still unknown.

If there is anything more noteworthy than the development of these structures and the speed with which these bony growths appear, it must be the remarkable way that they disappear. At the end of the reproductive season, in a couple of days the bony barbel vanishes and the spine reverts to a size similar to that of the female. Even the anal fin modifications appear less obvious at this time, so that males become almost indistinguishable from females.

A similar but less spectacular sexual dimorphism is found in the close relatives of the auchenipterids: the Centromochlidae. In all species of this family the male's anal fin is transformed into a rigid paddlelike structure that no longer functions as a fin. Instead, it is anchored in a bulbous mass of tissue that points almost directly backward instead of downward, as in females. At this time no one has observed how this modified fin is used in reproduction, but I suspect that it can be used to funnel sperm from the elongate genital tube of the male toward the newly released eggs of the female.

Reproductive Behavior

Much of what is known of the reproductive behavior of catfishes comes directly from observations made by hobbyists. Information about courtship, spawning, and, to a lesser degree, postspawning brood tending has only rarely been obtained from field observations. On the other hand, a large amount of indirect information on the reproductive biology of catfishes has been obtained from the field, using wild populations. Seasonality of reproduction and habitat preferences may not completely correlate with observations made on the same species in captivity, however, because the environmental cues that trigger reproductive behavior may be altered or altogether absent in aquarium situations. Thus, the combination of field and aquarium observations must be linked in order to piece together the whole story of reproduction in these fishes.

The range of reproductive activities and parental care exhibited by catfishes is startling. Within this one group of fishes we find species that give absolutely no care to their offspring and others that go so far as to carry their eggs around with them (in such varied places as their lower lip, belly, and mouth) or even arrange to have another species carry and orally incubate their eggs for them. While many catfishes leave the young to fend for themselves as soon as hatched, some species continue to guard the offspring and, more rarely, even find food for them. At least two species are known to produce a milk-colored skin secretion upon which the young feed.

What makes this diversity of reproductive activities even more fascinating is that the mode of reproduction of most catfishes, including a large number of families, is completely unknown at present. Much of what is known was discovered only within the past few decades. Thus, the array of activities that we know of now may be only the tip of the iceberg. In fact, the accounts given below are often from fragmentary reports on reproduction in the species listed. Because of the nature of observations in the field and in aquaria, it is not always possible to make them from courtship through to the development of young; therefore, placement of a species in one of the categories listed below may represent only a part of the care that is given by the parents. This is especially true for those species that have been observed to guard nests. Whether their guarding activities extend to the young is often unknown at present.

The range of parental care in catfishes can be broken down into groups, based on three criteria: presence and nature of a nest, tending of eggs, and care after hatching. With these criteria, the following patterns are found:
1. *No nest construction and no care of eggs or young.* The absence of any parental activity appears to be rare in catfishes but, curiously, the absence of care is well known to hobbyists. This is because many species of *Corydoras* and its close relatives, *Brochis* and *Aspidoris,* are included in this group.

In fishes of this category, eggs are generally fertilized by the male as they are released by the female, and are attached to aquatic vegetation by a sticky surface coating. The pair may spawn in the appropriate habitat and

74

the released eggs attach to the first structure with which they come in contact, or, in the case of many corys, the female may hold on to the eggs and deposit them on vegetation, a few at a time. For this, corys use their pelvic fins, which are cupped into a basket-like structure, to capture the eggs as they exit the genital pore and carry them around until an appropriate spot is located.

A spawning aggregation of *Corydoras paleatus*. Note that the pelvic fins of the large female (center) are clasped together into a basket. *Photo by:* A. van den Nieuwenhuizen.

A most curious variation on this is known for several species of *Corydoras,* including the commonly spawned *C. aeneus.* In this species the spawning pair release gametes during a spawning embrace, but instead of the sperm coming in contact with the eggs, the female gathers up sperm in her mouth. She then moves off alone to find a suitable spot for depositing the eggs that have collected in her pelvic fin basket. When a spot is chosen, the eggs are attached to the substrate and the sperm are re-leased onto the eggs, so that the eggs can be fertilized. A similar approach may be used by members of the family Auchenipteridae, but with yet another twist. Auchenipterids have an elaborate courtship that ends with internal insemination of the female. It is not yet known whether the eggs are fertilized inside the female, but it has been suggested that the female merely stores the sperm separately from the eggs. After copulation the female swims off, presumably in search of a suitable spot to deposit the eggs. At the time of the deposition the eggs are fertilized and begin development. It has been further suggested that the female may be able to store viable sperm in this manner for several months.

Only rarely have doradid catfish spawned under aquarium conditions. One species that has been bred successfully is *Agamyxis albomaculatus,* shown here. *Photo by:* J. O'Malley.

The extent of this mode of reproduction in catfishes is poorly known at present. In addition to the several species of *Corydoras* and, presumably, auchenipterids, reproduction without parental care was noted for at least one species of schilbid and the South American pimelodid *Brachyrhamdia imitator.* A recent article on the induced spawning of the spotted raphael, *Agamyxis albomaculatus,* gave no indication of parental care, but nest building has been reported for other species in this family. A few species of the Asian bagrids and African mochokids (of the genus *Synodontis*) have been reported to spawn in aquaria and scatter eggs widely, seemingly without further care.

2. *Nest building with egg guarding only.* To this category belong all catfishes that deposit their spawn in a limited area and guard (and usually tend) the eggs until the time of hatching or until the hatched fry are able to swim away from the nest. Thereafter, the fry seem to be on their own, with no support from the parents. Within this group there is a great amount of variation in terms of the nature of the nest and the parent that takes charge of guarding the eggs. In clariids and some silurids, eggs are deposited at the base of submerged vegetation, without any obvious effort by the parents to modify the site beforehand. The male guards the eggs in both of these groups. In the doradid *Amblydoras hancocki,* both parents guard a nest that consists of a pile of leaves, with the eggs sandwiched in between. The single species of Australian plotosid whose spawning has been observed, *Tandanus tandanus,* builds a nest of gravel and sticks in shallow places of a river bottom. Although both parents participate in nest building, the female leaves the area shortly after spawning, and only the male guards the nest.

An unusual form of nest building is exhibited by several callichthyids. Species of the genera *Callichthys,*

Hoplosternum, and *Dianema* all build floating nests of frothy bubbles and aquatic vegetation. The male constructs the nest by gulping air from the surface and emitting mucus-covered bubbles from his gill chamber. During spawning, the female catches newly released eggs in her pelvic fin pouch and deposits them on the lower surface of the bubble nest. The male adds more bubbles, pushing the eggs into the center of the nest, where they stay until the fry hatch out. Immediately after spawning, the female leaves the spawning site, and all guarding activities are the responsibility of the male alone.

Loricariids have a wide range of nest types. In all cases, however, it is only the males that guard the eggs, and females are usually chased away immediately after spawning. Plecos (genus *Hypostomus*) and the sailfin plecos (*Pterygoplichthys*) excavate holes in mudbanks along the shore and guard their eggs there. Bristle noses (genus *Ancistrus*) search out suitable shelter in caves, hollowed-out logs, or their equivalent (for example, inverted flower pots) to spawn. The long-tailed loricariids, often called whiptails, spawn on hard surfaces, often exposed, and do not seem to prepare the site to any extent. Whiptails are often quite specific about the nature of the surface, however, and seem uninterested in spawning if an appropriate surface is unavailable.

A specialized form of egg guarding, in which the eggs are carried around on the body of one parent, is exhibited by two groups of catfish. Males of several species of whiptail loricariids, including members of the genera *Pseudohemiodon* and *Loricariichthys,* carry a flattened plaque of eggs on the ventral surface of the elongated lower lip. The eggs are quite tightly bound together, but not to the male's lower lip. If disturbed, the plaque can be dislodged. I don't know if the parent will make any attempt to retrieve the eggs if dislodged. Long-tailed banjo cats also carry eggs on their belly, but the mechanism differs from that of loricariids in a number of ways. It is the female and not the male that carries the eggs, and the eggs are not attached together. Instead, each egg is attached to the swollen belly skin of the parent by a slender stalk. The stalk does more than just hold the egg in place: minute blood vessels extend into each stalk from an enlarged artery that appears on the ventral surface of the abdomen as the female becomes sexually mature. Although it has not been thoroughly studied, it appears that the vessels provide some nourishment to the developing embryo, in a manner similar to that of a mammalian placenta. It is not yet certain how the eggs become attached to the belly, but it has been suggested that the female rests on the newly spawned eggs and the eggs are cap-

An adult male *Loricariichthys* with a cluster of eggs attached to the surface of its lower lip. *Photo by: C. Ferraris.*

tured by the skin. Upon hatching, the fry appear to become independent of the mother, and the mother's abdomen returns to its nonreproductive state.

3. *Nest guarding with care given to eggs and young.* Care of the young is not common in fishes but has been reported for a number of catfish species. "Care" refers to the guarding of young catfishes for a period of time after the developing fry are free-swimming and may also include feeding the young.

The North American family Ictaluridae is probably best known for the care given by the parents. All species participate in post-hatching care of the young, and often both parents are involved. Spawning is undertaken over depressions in gravel or muddy substrates or, in the case of many

madtoms, under rocks and overhangs in the creek bed. Incidentally, beer cans and other similar human waste also seem to be attractive nesting sites for madtoms (not that providing additional nesting sites of this type should be encouraged). The eggs and fry are guarded by both parents in many bullhead species, although each sex seems to have a distinct role in the care of the young. Madtom fry, on the other hand, seem to be the responsibility of the male only, as the female leaves the nest shortly after depositing her eggs.

The Asian stinging cat, *Heteropneustes fossilis,* also guards its young until well after hatching. It has been reported that both parents construct a nest in a sandy bottom, and a clump of adhesive eggs is deposited. The nest and later the young are watched over by both parents for some period of time.

Males of the African bagrid *Bagrus meridionalis* have been observed watching over a cluster of the young

A cluster of *Loricariichthys* eggs. It is possible to see the eyes of the developing fishes through the transparent egg membrane. *Photo by:* C. Ferraris.

Adult female (*left*) and male *Loricariichthys*, showing sexual dimorphism in the development of the lower lip. *Photo by:* C. Ferraris.

as they feed from the bottom. It was suggested that the parent even participates in the search for food. Two species of Indian bagrid catfishes of the genus *Aorichthys* go one step further: the fry feed on a milky-looking substance that is exuded from the skin of the male that takes charge of guarding the brood, in a manner similar to that of discus and *Uaru,* of the family Cichlidae.

A specialized form of egg and fry guarding is seen in the family Ariidae. All ariids (with one possible exception) brood their eggs orally. The newly released eggs are apparently held in a basketlike structure formed by the pelvic fins of the female. They are thought to be fertilized there and then transferred to the mouth of the male. The male maintains the eggs throughout the entire incubation period and the fry well after they hatch. Unfortunately, the actual care of eggs and fry has not been observed, so it is not known for sure whether the fry are able to move into and out of the oral cavity, as is done in many cichlids.

An interesting modification of oral brooding has recently come to light. The Lake Tanganyika mochokid *Synodontis multipunctatus* has its eggs orally brooded, but not by the parents. Instead, the eggs are released into the water column while one or more species of oral-brooding cichlids are in the throes of a spawning bout. In the process of gathering up her own eggs for incubation, the female cichlid must also take in some of the catfish eggs, and thereby begin to brood them as well. The catfish eggs develop and hatch inside the mouth of the cichlid, and fully formed miniature *S. multipunctatus* eventually emerge. It has been suggested that the catfishes not only receive shelter during this period but may also partake of their first meals in the form of cichlid eggs or fry.

Synodontis multipunctatus is the only catfish known to transfer the responsibilities of egg rearing to another species. *Photo by:* M. Smith.

Quite recently a new twist to this story has developed. One aquarist who successfully bred multipuncs together with Lake Malawi cichlids noticed that after several spawnings, the catfishes no longer timed their spawnings to match the cichlids'. Instead, they freely spawned and scattered their eggs along the substrate, in the absence of cichlids. There is no evidence that this occurs in the same manner in Lake Tanganyika, where one researcher looked in vain for free *Synodontis* eggs or fry.

Within the past few years the number of catfishes that have been spawned in captivity has increased greatly. This is due to both the number of catfish available to aquarists and the increased efforts to induce spawning activity in various species. There have been some noteworthy successes in this regard, which have contributed to the availability of species otherwise rare in the hobby. At the same time, there are a number of catfish species that have resisted all hobbyist attempts to induce spawning.

Catfishes of the World

There are about 2500 species of catfish worldwide. At present they are divided into thirty-three families, each containing one to more than six hundred species. Nineteen of these catfish families include species that are kept routinely as aquarium fishes. Species in several of the other families can be found also, with a bit of searching. The large number of catfishes that can be thought of as aquarium fishes makes it impossible to do justice to all of them here. In an attempt to summarize who's who in catfishes, I have taken the approach of briefly describing the family, with more detailed notes on some of the commonly available species or those of special interest. In some ways this is not an entirely satisfactory approach. Some families are quite small and not of any particular importance to aquarists. Others, such as the Loricariidae and Pimelodidae, are large and full of species that make excellent additions to catfish hobbyists' aquaria. Families such as these deserve much more space than I can give them here. Perhaps a separate book is in order.

I chose to include all of the catfish families for one simple reason: no one knows what catfishes will appear in the aquarium trade in the future. If you are lucky enough to discover a really unusual catfish, you must begin the process of identifying your find somewhere. Each of the family accounts that follows has a brief summary of the important anatomical features that are useful for identifying members of that family. Once you know what family your catfish belongs to, determining its species becomes easier (but not always easy). Within the past few years

alone, species in several families of catfish have arrived that were rarely, if ever, previously seen in the aquarium hobby.

Each of the following family accounts includes a summary of what is known about the biology of the catfishes, especially relating to aquarium life. Special aspects of water conditions, feeding, and reproduction are included, if known, as well as information on the natural distribution of the family. This is essential to have if you want to search for more information on your fishes. Most fish books are organized by region, and without knowing which continent (at least) your catfish comes from, it is virtually impossible to gather any additional knowledge about the fish.

The families are listed alphabetically in two groups. The first nineteen families are those most commonly seen in the aquarium hobby. Most likely, a "new" catfish will be a member of one of these. The families listed at the end of the chapter are quite rare in the aquarium hobby. If you are fortunate enough to find and maintain a fish from any of these families, you would be doing your fellow hobbyists a service by writing an article about your find (see the chapter "Beyond This Book").

Common Catfish Families

Ariidae
(*air EE id dee*)

The Ariidae are one of the few catfish families that have both marine and

The shark cat, *Arius jordani,* can quickly grow to a large size and outgrow its welcome in an aquarium. *Photo by:* P. Loiselle.

freshwater inhabitants. They are often referred to as "sea catfish," because they are so often found in near-shore marine waters. In the aquarium hobby they are sometimes referred to as "shark catfish," because of their graceful sharklike swimming and perpetual motion. In addition, their prominent dorsal and pectoral fins add to the sharklike appearance of the young ones that are most commonly seen in pet stores.

The body form of ariids is exactly what I think of as a "typical" catfish: the skin is always smooth and naked, the dorsal and pectoral fins sport prominent spines with sharp tips, and the snout is surrounded by three pairs of elongated barbels. Another way of saying this is that ariids seem to lack any superficial traits that can be used to easily distinguish them from other families of catfishes. Instead, ariids can be recognized by a combination of

traits: no nasal barbel (three pairs of barbels); dorsal fin just behind the head and with an elongate platelike bone between the head and the dorsal fin spine; large pectoral fins with a strong spine; caudal fin strongly forked; body without plates or spines and often silvery or gray in color, rarely with markings except on fins.

Ariids are the only catfishes that have a worldwide distribution. Species can be found in tropical and subtropical marine and brackish waters of all continents and in freshwater lakes and rivers in most of the tropics. Of the more than 100 species in the family, only a very few have been kept in aquaria. Those that can be found in pet shops in the United States come from the west coast of Central America and western Ecuador, under the names *Arius seemani* and *A. jordani.* Quite possibly, there are several species that arrive from these localities under these names. They are usually sold at a young age, at 2 to 4 inches in length. They thrive in a community aquarium and grow quickly (often at the expense of their tankmates) to more than 12 inches long. The growing fish lose the very attractive black velvet color of their fins, and the fish become a uniform silvery gray.

Because of the large size attained by the adults, they are rarely seen in captivity outside of public aquaria. This is unfortunate, as the family exhibits a form of reproduction that is unique among catfishes, and the details of the spawning behavior remain a mystery. Male ariids practice oral incubation of both eggs and young fish. During spawning season, male sea catfish can be found swimming with a mouthful of eggs, yolk sac fry, or both. The sequence of steps that ultimately leads to the male's holding the eggs is unknown. In many species, mature females grow a fleshy pad on their pelvic fins. It has been suggested that this pad holds newly laid eggs for the male to take into his mouth, but several questions remain unanswered: Does the male take the eggs one at a time or in batches? Does the male take eggs from more than one female? How do males obtain eggs from females that don't grow these fleshy pads?

These and the many other unanswered questions about the reproductive biology of ariid catfishes will be answered only when adults are kept in captivity. The generally turbid waters that ariids generally call home preclude any hope of observation in nature, leaving large home aquaria and, more likely, public aquaria as the sources from which information on these fishes will come.

The highly fused neurocranium and anterior vertebral column of ariid catfishes lend themselves to religious art. *Photo by:* C. Ferraris.

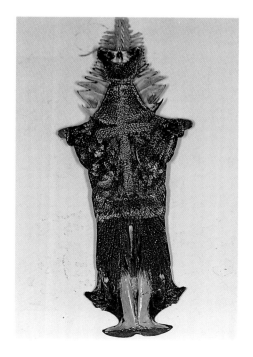

Even the dorsal surface of the neurocranium was dressed up in this work of art. *Photo by:* C. Ferraris.

Aspredinidae

(*az pra DIN id dee*)

Banjo catfishes and their relatives are collectively known as the family Aspredinidae. There seems little question of where the name "banjo catfish" comes from: the flattened disk-shaped body attached to a long slender tail resembles a banjo quite well. For similar reasons, the name "frying-pan cat" has also been used for these fishes. Members of the family can be recognized easily by this peculiar shape, the absence of an adipose dorsal fin, and the presence of horizontal rows of small conical bumps that line the body surface. Only the extremely rare Asian catfish family Akysidae can be confused with banjos, but akysids almost always have prominent adipose fins.

Aspredinids come from tropical South America, where they are widely

One of the long-tailed banjo catfishes, *Aspredo cotylophorus,* showing the many-rayed anal fin from which it got its name. *Photo by:* P. Loiselle.

distributed through the continent. Two groups are recognized by scientists and hobbyists alike. One, containing the typical banjos, has a comparatively short tail, with an anal fin that is about the same size as the head. These fishes, which I call the "*Bunocephalus* banjos," are the only aspredinids routinely found in the aquarium hobby. All members of this group come from freshwater forest streams and rivers. As many as twenty-five species are known, but the taxonomy of the group is so confused at present that the correct assignment of a species name to an individual can seldom be done. Most species are small, rarely exceeding 4 inches in total length. Usually those found in the hobby belong to the genus *Dysichthys* (recently transferred to that genus from the better-known name *Bunocephalus*), which can be recognized by the flattened head without a prominent ridge. Occasionally craggy-headed banjos, now placed in the genus *Bunocephalus* (formerly *Agmus*), are found. Even more rarely is the truly bizarre *Amaralia hypsiura* seen. One need see only the promi-

nent vertical bony projections on the caudal region to recognize this fish. At least three other genera are recognized, but none of these has yet made it into the aquarium hobby.

The second group of aspredinids are the long-tailed banjos, unmistakably identified by the elongate caudal region with an anal fin of more than fifty rays. Only four species are known, and, unlike the *Bunocephalus* banjos, the long-tailed banjos inhabit the mouths of rivers in northern South America which are typically estuarine.

Banjo catfishes of the genus *Dysichthys* can be extremely flat, leaving only the dorsal fin extending much above the substratum. *Photo by:* C. Ferraris.

The skin of all banjo catfishes is covered with regular rows of bumps (called papillae) that seem to form lines running from head to tail. *Photo by:* C. Ferraris.

The bumpy ridge running from the dorsal fin to the tail of *Amaralia hypsiura* makes this species readily recognizable. *Photo by:* W. Foersch.

Unfortunately, they are only rarely seen in the hobby and have the reputation of being difficult to keep alive. This is probably due to their being thought of as freshwater fishes and placed in water containing little or no salt. They do quite well in brackish water tanks, and captive spawning of these fishes is probably not far off.

All banjo catfish are lethargic and nocturnal. Most species spend the daylight hours buried beneath sand or leaf litter and emerge from hiding only at night or, with some training, for food. Because of their habit of burying themselves, a fine sand substrate is better for them than the more generally used coarse gravel.

Two peculiarities about aspredinids are worth mentioning here. The first is the peculiar mode of locomotion they employ at times. When startled, they can jet-propel themselves over the substrate by pumping water through their gill slits. This causes a jerky, hopping movement, as each spurt of water moves the fish only a short distance.

The second peculiarity involves a skin shedding that is curiously like that of snakes and other reptiles but is known to occur in only a few fishes. Large, thin sheets of epidermal coating of a fish will slough off the body and settle on the substrate. In extreme cases, the nearly complete surface coat of a fish will rest, intact, on the bottom of the tank. More frequently, bits and pieces of skin can be found scattered across the surface of the substrate. This skin must be tasty, as it disappears quite rapidly in community tanks, even to the point of being picked off the catfish by an exceptionally hungry tankmate. Only in tanks that contain banjos exclusively can this unusual activity be observed. The quick elimination of the evidence helps explain how this skin sloughing escaped notice until quite recently, even though banjo cats have been kept in aquaria for decades.

Little is known about the reproductive biology of banjo catfish. *Bunocephalus* banjos have only rarely been spawned in captivity. The long-tailed banjos have what is thought to be a unique system of care for the eggs. Eggs are attached to the ventral surface of the female's abdomen by a thin stalk that contains minute blood vessels extending from a large abdominal vein of the adult. Apparently, the embryos are nourished by this blood supply until hatching. This is thought to be the only occurrence of maternal nourishment of embryos in catfishes, and one of only a very few cases known in fishes. This most unusual form of parental care may be related to the estuarine habitat from which all long-tailed banjos come. The muddy bottoms of most estuaries provide little firm substrate for nest construction, and eggs deposited on the bottom are likely to be covered with silt and suffocate. It is noteworthy that

the other catfish family found routinely in estuaries, the Ariidae, also carry their embryos rather than placing them in nests.

Auchenipteridae
(*ow ken ip TARE id dee*)

Mode of reproduction sets the Neotropical family Auchenipteridae apart from all other catfishes. Only members of this family undergo internal insemination and fertilization. Associated with this unique reproductive pattern is a pronounced sexual dimorphism that is rivaled only by that of certain members of the Loricariidae.

Auchenipterids rarely exceed 6 inches in length, although a few species of *Ageneiosus,* formerly placed in

Craggy-headed banjo catfishes were formerly included in the genus *Agmus.* Now they are placed in *Bunocephalus. Photo by:* C. Ferraris.

the family Ageneiosidae, reach more than a foot in length. Most species are shy and nocturnal, rarely venturing out of hiding during the day. The daytime residence is generally a crevice in rockwork or wood, often of a size that seems impossibly small when compared with that of the fish itself. The name "wood cats," which is often used for this family, refers to the habits of some species as well as the somber earthy coloration found in many species.

Auchenipterids are known in Panama and throughout tropical South America. Currently, only a few of the approximately seventy-five species are routinely found in the aquarium trade, but many more appear irregularly and in small numbers as contaminants in shipments of other catfishes.

Distinguishing auchenipterids from

The name wood catfish seems particularly appropriate for some auchenipterids, such as this member of the genus *Trachelyopterus,* which looks somewhat like a piece of driftwood. *Photo by:* P. Loiselle.

other catfishes is not always easy. Many species resemble members of the closely related Doradidae and Centromochlidae. All of these families are characterized by a nuchal shield that consists of a series of bony plates extending from the top of the skull to the beginning of the dorsal fin. Almost all species have a curious pattern of white dots that run in vertical rows along the sides of the body. The dots are part of a superficial sensory organ called the lateral line. The dots are often obscured by the bolder color patterning of the body, but can be seen with a little effort. In addition, all auchenipterids lack nasal barbels, as do their close relatives the centromochlids and doradids.

Auchenipterids differ from the others by having modifications of the genital pores of both males and females. The genital pore of males extends along the anterior edge of the anal fin, so that the opening is at the tip of the fin. Usually the fin rays that support this tubular pore are thickened and elongated, forming a structure similar to the gonopodium of guppies and

A continuous layer of bone extends from behind the eyes to the dorsal spine in auchenipterids and a few other families of catfishes. Photo by: J. O'Malley.

other poeciliids. The female's genital pore is enlarged and recessed into her abdomen, leaving a conspicuous indentation into which the male's gonopodium is inserted during copulation.

These reproductive structures are found only in adult auchenipterids, of course. Identifying juvenile fishes is somewhat difficult unless the species is a familiar one. They can always be distinguished from doradids by the lack of bony plates along the sides of the body in the latter family. Centromochlids are more difficult to distinguish, and small ones can be easily misidentified unless a close look is taken. Most auchenipterids have a long anal fin base, sufficient to distinguish them from centromochlids and doradids, both of which have anal fins that are no longer than their dorsal fins. The rare jaguar and black-jaguar cats are the only auchenipterids with small anal fins. Fortunately, these species are very distinctive and cannot be easily mistaken for any other.

The most commonly seen au-

chenipterid in the aquarium trade is a species of *Auchenipterichthys*, often called a "midnight" or "zamora cat." Occasionally a very attractive spotted form of this genus appears, but in small numbers. The most spectacular species of auchenipterid imported is the jaguar cat, *Liosomadoras oncinus*. Only a few years ago this species was unknown in the hobby and a scientific rarity, but in recent years it has been imported regularly, although seasonally, into the American market. Jaguars are somewhat difficult to keep initially, for reasons that are still a mystery, but those that survive seem to do quite well in captivity.

Most often the name "wood cat" is used for members of the genus *Trachelyopterus* (formerly called *Parauchenipterus* or *Trachycorystes*). Several species of these shy and retiring

89

Although *Trachelyichthys exilis* is only rarely available in the aquarium hobby, it is a most attractive addition to a community aquarium. *Photo by:* P. Loiselle.

The midnight, or zamora, catfish (*Auchenipterichthys thoracatus*) is both peaceful and graceful: two important characteristics for a community aquarium resident. *Photo by:* P. Loiselle.

Young individuals of the jaguar catfish, *Liosomadoras oncinus,* have a bold color pattern. *Photo by:* C. Ferraris.

The color pattern of mature jaguar catfish is not as bold as it is in juveniles, but it is still one of the most striking patterns found in catfish. *Photo by:* C. Ferraris.

The black jaguar, *Trachycorystes trachycorystes,* grows to a much larger size than does the more commonly available jaguar catfish. *Photo by:* C. Ferraris.

Although it looks quite similar to other wood cats, *Trachelyopterus coriaceus* can be distinguished from all other species by the absence of an adipose fin. *Photo by:* C. Ferraris.

fishes can be found in the hobby, but distinguishing species takes a close look and a practiced eye. One of the most graceful catfish found in the aquarium hobby is the mandube cat, *Trachelyopterichthys taeniatus.* Mandube cats are only rarely imported from their home in the Brazilian Amazon, and then they are likely to come in as part of a shipment consisting of several auchenipterid and centromochlid species.

The mandube catfish, *Trachelyopterichthys taeniatus,* swims with a graceful, eel-like motion. *Photo by:* C. Ferraris.

The peculiar reproductive strategy of auchenipterids is often manifested in elaborate, dimorphic secondary sexual characteristics otherwise not known in catfishes. During reproductive season the male's dorsal spine becomes elongate and/or ornamented with fine spines. Afterward these bony structures return to a state that is no different from that of the female. In a number of species, including members of the genera *Auchenipterus, Ageneiosus, Entomacorus,* and *Trachelyopterus,* the otherwise flexible maxillary barbel is transformed into a stiffened bony rod, which in species of *Ageneiosus* is studded with stout, recurved spines. As with the dorsal fin spine, barbels revert to their nonbony condition at the end of the reproductive season.

In courtship, males use the barbel and dorsal fin spine to firmly grasp the female behind the head, thereby immobilizing her during intromission. The spawning clasp in *Ageneiosus* may last for several minutes, during which the male maintains a firm hold of his mate.

Feeding auchenipterids is not a problem, though their feeding behavior may come as a surprise at first. Nocturnal cats, they seem reluctant to feed in a brightly lit tank, at least initially. Like many other catfishes, most species do seem to overcome their aversion to light long enough to feed. Quite unlike most catfishes, however, many auchenipterids will quickly head to the surface of the aquarium for food. Floating insects seem to be a major food source in nature, so the transition to flakes or floating pellets appears to be an easy one for them to make. They seem to have no limit to the amount of food they will consume, and they will aggressively compete with tankmates for available food.

93

This attractive species was only recently given the name *Ageneiosus magoi*. Adult females and sexually inactive males look very much alike and can be distinguished only upon close examination. *Photo by:* C. Ferraris.

A sexually active male *Ageneiosus magoi*. Note the marked increase in length of the dorsal fin spine and the remarkable thickening of the anterior margin of the anal fin. These two transformations are characteristic of adult male auchenipterids. *Photo by:* P. Loiselle.

Bagridae

(*BAG rid dee*)

The Bagridae are a large and diverse catfish family found throughout Africa and Asia. Bagrids are important food fishes wherever they are found, as many species grow to large sizes. A few species are well-known aquarium fishes, and several others are rarely imported but are greatly sought by aquarists.

Bagrids are often referred to as generalized catfishes because of their lack of unusual structural features to help set them apart from other catfish families. It has been suggested that several other families descended from bagrids or bagrid-like catfishes. The lack of remarkable features to distinguish bagrids makes it difficult to easily recognize all of the species that are routinely placed in the family. There are, however, some guidelines that will usually work to identify a catfish as a bagrid. Members of this family always have naked skin, never with bony plates or scutes. Three or four pairs of barbels are always present. The nasal barbels are often absent, but those species that have barbels can readily be distinguished from the Neotropical Pimelodidae, in which nasal barbels are always lacking. The maxillary barbels are rarely very long, unlike the barbels in a number of pimelodids, which trail well beyond the head of the fish and often to the tail or beyond. The anal fin is usually small when compared with other families with pronounced anal fins, such as ictalurids, auchenipterids, schilbids, and silurids. Often the anal fin is about the same size as or even much smaller than the adipose dorsal fin, which is often in the form of an elongated ridge of tissue

An Indian bagrid, *Chandramara chandramara.* Note the very short maxillary barbels that are characteristic of this species. Unlike most bagrids, *Chandramara* seems most at home in groups. *Photo by:* P. Loiselle.

that runs between the dorsal fin and the tail. Sometimes the anal fin and the adipose fin are nearly equal in size and appear to be symmetrical above and below the body of the fish. Strong, sharply pointed spines are found at the front of both the dorsal and pectoral fins of bagrids. The dorsal fin is always situated just behind the head and never dominates the dorsal profile, as it does in many loricariid and clariid catfish.

Beyond these characteristics, the diversity of body shapes found in the family defies simplification. It often seems that bagrids are identified as such when they don't fit neatly into any other family of catfishes.

At present there are more than 200 known species in the Bagridae. Quite a number of species can be found in the aquarium hobby, but most of these are rare imports that cannot be found routinely. In fact, only two or three species are widely available at present, including the Asian bumblebee cat, *Leiocassis siamensis,* and the two-spot catfish, *Mystus micracanthus.* Both of these species are relatively small and can be included in community aquaria of larger fishes. Of the African Bagridae, only the giraffe cats, of the genus *Auchenoglanis,* can be considered common fishes for the aquarium hobby, but even these are difficult to find.

Bagrids are almost always predatory fishes and must be kept away from anything that is small enough to swallow. Most species can be trained relatively easily to eat prepared foods, especially sinking pelletized food. Although they appear similar to pimelodids, only rarely do I hear of any bagrid being kept as a pet and being as responsive as a red-tailed or sailfin pimelodid. This may be due in part to the high cost of some of the larger species, or it may simply be a difference in personality of these fishes.

The two-spot catfish, *Mystus micracanthus,* is the most commonly available species of bagrid. *Photo by:* P. Loiselle.

Some of the more attractive bagrid species are quite aggressive toward each other and must be kept apart. A good example of this is the black lancer, *Bagrichthys macracanthus* (sometimes identified as *B. hypselop-terus*). It seems that under no conditions can more than one of these live peacefully in a reasonably sized aquarium. Inevitably a newcomer to a tank is welcomed with such a severe thrashing on its first night that survival is almost always in doubt. Until the solution to this problem is overcome, it would appear that successful aquarium spawnings of these fishes are unlikely.

Conditions necessary for the successful keeping of bagrids may be as diverse as the family. Many species seem to be able to tolerate a wide range of conditions and do quite well in aquaria set up as community tanks. There are reported cases, however, of species that have very specific requirements, at least during the transition period from the wild to captive liv-

Parauchenoglanis guttatus is a small member of the giraffe catfish group of bagrids, all of which are native to Africa. *Photo by:* M. Smith.

ing. Again, the black lancer is a good example. Lancers died off in great numbers when they were first imported into the United States. Only relatively recently has their mortality gone down. It was discovered that they do not do well in cool water, at least initially. When placed in warmer water (85 degrees or more) for a few days after arrival and then slowly acclimated to more normal temperatures, they seem to take the transition much better. They may do quite well, in fact, in constantly warmer water, but initially at least they need the extra heat. Experimentation of this kind may lead to other breakthroughs in keeping unusual bagrids.

Little is known about the reproductive biology of bagrids. What little has been reported shows this family to have the potential to reveal many new

The Asian red-tailed catfish, *Mystus nemurus,* is one of the few large bagrids that can be found in the aquarium trade. *Photo by:* P. Loiselle.

The black lancer (*Bagrichthys macracanthus*), a species found throughout Southeast Asia, must be kept warm and well fed when first obtained if it is to have any chance of becoming acclimated to an aquarium. *Photo by:* J. O'Malley.

The harlequin lancer (*Bagroides melapterus*) from Borneo, a relative newcomer to the aquarium hobby, behaves very much like its close relative the black lancer. Photo by: J. O'Malley.

and interesting variations in catfish biology. For example, at least three species of Asian bagrids, *Aorichthys aor, A. seenghala,* and *Mystus gulio,* undergo a transformation in the belly skin of breeding adults. The skin becomes soft and spongy and is supplied with a large number of blood vessels. While guarding the newly hatched fry, the parents secrete a whitish substance from their belly skin, on which the young feed. This behavior is quite reminiscent of the larval feeding behavior of the discus (*Symphysodon* spp.) in the family Cichlidae. It has also been suggested that newly laid eggs attach to the softened underbelly of these fishes and are nourished until hatching with the blood supply of the parent, similar to what is found in the long-tailed banjo catfishes. Although these species are not common aquarium fish (and the two species of *Aorichthys* never will be, because when they mature they are in excess of 4 feet), it is entirely possible that this behavior occurs in other species that

could be raised in aquarium conditions. Verifying and observing the details of this relationship between parent and offspring would certainly add to the ever-growing repertoire of reproductive behaviors exhibited by catfishes.

Callichthyidae
(*kal ik THEE id dee*)

The family Callichthyidae is probably the best known group of catfishes among aquarium fish keepers. The popularity of the species of *Corydoras,* the largest genus of the family, is well justified. Almost all members of the genus are peaceful, hardy aquarium residents that add color and activity to any community tank. In addition, some corys are easily bred and are often the first catfishes that hobbyists rear.

But callichthyids include much more than just *Corydoras*. The family includes a number of species that only vaguely resemble *Corydoras* in both appearance and behavior. What makes this diversity all the more fascinating is that nearly all species are potential candidates for the aquarium hobby, if only they can be obtained.

Callichthyids can be readily recognized by the presence of two rows of overlapping bony plates that cover the body. In addition, all species possess a barbel at each corner of the mouth, the rictal barbel, that is often as large as or larger than the maxillary barbel. Callichthyids have the ability to supplement their oxygen intake by gulping atmospheric air and swallowing it into their guts. The swallowed bubble of air

Note the scalelike appearance of the overlapping bony plates in this *Corydoras haraldschultzi. Photo by:* J. O'Malley.

is trapped in an enlarged, thin-walled portion of the gut, where oxygen is removed in exchange for carbon dioxide. When the oxygen content of the bubble is depleted, the bubble is expelled and another is swallowed. This process allows callichthyids to survive in waters with little dissolved oxygen and to increase their oxygen consumption during periods of stress. Often, corys and sailfin corys (genus *Brochis*) will surface in groups and gulp air in unison. In one part of the Rio Ucayali drainage of Peru, groups of fifty or more were seen surfacing at regular intervals. It has been suggested that this group activity may confuse the numerous predatory birds (such as kingfishers, which are incredibly abundant along the shores of most South and Central American streams and rivers) that haunt the area for food.

The family can be divided into two groups, based on the shape of the head. Members of the genera *Corydoras, Brochis,* and miniature corys

Two pairs of barbels are found at the corner of the mouth in *Corydoras* and all other genera of the family Callichthyidae. *Photo by:* W. de Graaf.

(genus *Aspidoras*) all have strongly compressed heads, with the depth of the head being much greater than the width. In contrast, the genera *Callichthys, Hoplosternum,* and *Dianema* have depressed, flattened heads and are generally more elongate fishes.

The more than 100 species of callichthyids come from tropical South America and the island of Trinidad. The largest species, belonging to the genera *Hoplosternum* and *Callichthys,* grow to no more than about 8 inches. In contrast, some species of *Aspidoras* and *Corydoras* mature at just over an inch.

The comparative ease with which some callichthyids are kept and bred in captivity has made it possible to document the reproductive biology of these fishes to a much greater extent than for any other catfish family. As with the head shape, the patterns of reproduction fall into two neat groups. The depressed-headed callichthyids, namely *Callichthys, Hoplosternum,* and *Dianema,* all show a behavior that

is apparently unique in catfishes: bubble nest building. A frothy nest of bubbles and plant matter is closely tended and guarded by the male. The complicated courtship ritual between the spawning pair culminates in the deposit of eggs on the lower surface of the nest, after which the female is unceremoniously invited to leave the area quickly. Eggs and embryos develop in the nest under the watchful eyes of the male.

In contrast, reproduction in *Corydoras* and the other compressed-headed species is done without bubble nests or male parental care of the developing offspring but is nonetheless peculiar. After courtship, eggs are released from the female's ovary a few at a time and caught in her pelvic fins, which have been brought together into a basketlike structure. The adhesive

Members of the genus *Brochis* are readily recognized by the large number of rays in the dorsal fin. *Photo by:* J. O'Malley.

Species of the genus *Aspidoras* look very much like *Corydoras*, but note how small the eyes of this fish are. *Photo by:* P. Loiselle.

Hoplosternum pectorale, one of two species of the genus that are readily available in the hobby, is easily distinguished by its shallowly forked caudal fin. *Photo by:* J. O'Malley.

The adult male *Hoplosternum pectorale* develops an elongated, thickened pectoral spine that is turned up at the tip. *Photo by:* J. O'Malley.

eggs are generally fertilized at that point and carried off by the female to be deposited either in vegetation or on firm vertical surfaces such as rocks or the walls of an aquarium. Some reports suggest, however, that the eggs of some species are not fertilized immediately after release from the ovary but only at the time of deposit on their substrate, and in a most unusual manner. After a spawning bout, the female breaks away from the male and searches for a suitable place to release the eggs that are gathering into her pelvic fins. Then the female fertilizes the eggs with sperm that she previously gathered in her mouth from her male partner. The sperm are then discharged onto either the deposited eggs or the substrate, followed by the eggs.

Keeping callichthyids in the aquarium is quite easy for most species. With only a few exceptions, they are very peaceful when kept in groups and in community tank situations. Most of these fishes tolerate a wide variety of aquarium conditions and will thrive with minimal care. Their easy maintenance should not deter the advanced aquarist from keeping these fishes, however. The reproductive behavior of these fishes is quite varied, and much is still unknown.

Note the squared-off margin of the caudal fin that is characteristic of *Hoplosternum thoracatum. Photo by:* P. Loiselle.

Corydoras robineae, called the "flag-tailed cory" because of its conspicuously marked caudal fin, is one of the more recent arrivals to the aquarium hobby. *Photo by:* J. O'Malley.

Many species of *Corydoras* have rows of black spots covering their bodies. Identification of these multispotted species can be quite difficult. *Photo by:* P. Loiselle.

Even at 2 inches in length, this young *Corydoras barbatus* shows the characteristic color pattern of adults. *Photo by:* J. O'Malley.

Centromochlidae
(*sen tro MOAK lid dee*)

Centromochlids had been considered members of the family Auchenipteridae until recently. Unlike auchenipterids, however, centromochlids are thought not to undergo internal fertilization, and they do not have the sexual dimorphism of the dorsal fin spine that characterizes auchenipterids.

About thirty-five species, belonging to the genera *Tatia, Glanidium,* and *Centromochlus,* are known at present. All come from tropical South America. Unlike auchenipterids, none are known to occur in Central America or west of the Andes Mountains. Rarely do any centromochlids grow larger than 5 inches, and several species

mature at 2 inches.

Centromochlids can be recognized by the presence of a continuous shield of bone covering the area between the head and dorsal spine and by a short, small anal fin. All species lack nasal barbels and lateral body scutes, and they have a tiny adipose dorsal fin. As with auchenipterids, centromochlids readily feed at the surface of the water and extend their maxillary barbels upward, touching the water surface.

At present, one or two species of the genus *Tatia* are about the only centromochlids to be seen in the hobby. *Tatia* can be recognized because the region between the anal fin and caudal fin is about the same depth as the more anterior parts of the body. In all other centromochlids and in catfishes in general, the region just anterior to the caudal fin is markedly reduced in depth compared to the rest of the body. This region, the caudal peduncle, is broadest in mature males, which also have an asymmetric caudal fin, with the upper portion longer than the lower. *Tatia* species are found

An adult male *Tatia*. As in all males of the family Centromochlidae, the anal fin is out on a short stalk. Compare this with the position of the anal fin of a female of the same species, in the following photograph. *Photo by:* P. Loiselle.

An adult female *Tatia*. *Photo by:* P. Loiselle.

A species of the genus *Tatia.* Note how the barbels of this fish are arched upward. *Photo by:* C. Ferraris.

throughout the range of the family, but those that have been arriving in the American aquarium trade have been coming from the lower and middle Amazon River, under the name "cunchi cats." Unfortunately, that name is also used for several different species of auchenipterids, so blindly obtaining fish under this name may not get you what you expect.

Sexual dimorphism exists in all centromochlid species and is readily apparent in all but a few. The anal fin of adult males is transformed into a stiffened, backwardly pointed structure that may help to clasp the female during reproductive activities. The entire anal fin is at the tip of a short cylindrical stalk that further emphasizes the difference between males and females.

Unfortunately, at present nothing is known about reproduction in this family. It is hoped that, should anyone be fortunate enough to observe a spawning, a thorough account of the activities will be written up for publication.

Chacidae
(*CHA sid dee*)

Species of the Asian family Chacidae must be considered among the most interesting of all known catfishes. The peculiar form and habits of these fish make them unlike any other family. They are some of the true oddballs in catfishdom.

The chacids consist of one genus with three species. *Chaca chaca,* the first species known, is said to have received its name from the sound that it made when removed from the water. Curiously, *C. bankanensis,* the only species of this family that is generally available to aquarists, is silent when taken out of water, which left me in doubt as to the validity of the origin of the name. Recently, however, I had the opportunity to see some *C. chaca,* and, true to their legend, they quickly and continuously bellowed their name.

Chacids can be recognized readily by the unmistakable shape of their body. The broadly flattened, squared-off head and gaping mouth set them off from all other catfishes. They also have a broadly rounded caudal fin that extends anteriorly to nearly above the anal fin.

In addition to their curious morphology, there are several behavioral peculiarities that characterize the species of this family. *Chaca* has been called the "angler catfish" for its ability to attract potential food to within striking distance of its mouth by movement of its maxillary barbels. The small, almost insignificant barbels that are found on the sides of the capacious mouth can perform in a fashion that is reminiscent of several marine angler fishes but is otherwise unknown in catfishes. At times the barbels can be wiggled, bringing life to an otherwise

motionless catfish. Small though they are, their movement is especially noticeable in contrast to the apparent lifeless body to which they are attached. The movement was more than sufficient to catch my eye, and it presumably does equally well on small fishes. I've been told that newly imported specimens of *Chaca* are more apt to use their maxillary barbel lure than are fish that have been kept in captivity for a long time. It seems they may learn that in captivity food fishes will swim close by without the angling, making it unnecessary to expend any energy. The second behavior of note is the jet-propulsive form of locomotion that these fishes utilize. The broad, paddlelike tail of *Chaca* works admirably well to move the fish along while unobstructed. But when resistance is encountered, *Chaca* changes to its second form of movement, jet

Chaca bankanensis, the frog-mouth catfish from Southeast Asia. *Photo by:* C. Ferraris.

propulsion. By forcing water from the mouth and gill chamber through a very restricted opercular opening, *Chaca* generates a force not unlike that of airplane jets. With the very large oral cavity that characterizes these fishes, a force sufficient to move the fish can be achieved. When stuck or held firmly in place, *Chaca* will repeatedly expel water in this fashion until it is freed.

As with many predatory catfishes, *Chaca* can consume surprisingly large prey. Given its extraordinarily large mouth, there are few fishes that could even remotely be considered as tankmates, and most *Chaca* keepers wisely devote a single tank to these fishes. They move only infrequently and for short distances, so a small tank is not out of the question. Feeding *Chaca* is a straightforward proposition: live fish or nothing. Goldfish seem most appropriate, but other live fishes,

such as baitfish (shiners, minnows, etc.), can be used. Curiously, guppies do not fare well in *Chaca* tanks. After browsing on the skin of *Chaca,* which looks, after all, like a moss-covered log, guppies almost always die. This may be due to a toxic secretion on the surface of *Chaca* skin, but this has yet to be investigated.

Nothing is known about reproduction in *Chaca.* Even distinguishing males from females has yet to be documented. *C. bankanensis* matures at about 6 inches, making it a most suitable size for an aquarium spawning. Indeed, several specimens of that size were found to have fully developed, ripe ovaries, but without ever showing any indication of reproductive activity. Although keeping *Chaca* may involve a somewhat hefty feeder-goldfish bill, the prospect of observing the breeding of these amazing fishes should lure some enthusiast to find the right conditions to stimulate *Chaca* to spawn.

The mouth of a frog-mouth catfish is capable of opening to a tremendous size. *Photo by:* S. Ferraris.

Clariidae
(*klair, EE id dee*)

The family Clariidae includes the infamous walking catfishes that have become naturalized in south Florida and are causing alarm for the welfare of native fishes there. The name "walking catfish" comes from the ability and willingness of some of these fishes to travel overland in search of a different place to call home.

Clariids are native to both Asia and Africa, with more than 100 species known at present. The family is one of the easiest to recognize, as its members possess several characteristics that are unique among catfishes. The most readily noticeable is the elongated dorsal fin that lacks a spine. In most species of the family the dorsal fin extends from just behind the head to the caudal fin, and they are even sometimes connected. A few species have a long, fleshy adipose fin between the dorsal fin and the caudal fin.

In every shipment of frog-mouth catfish, some have white eyes, as seen here. This is not an indication that the fish are unhealthy; perhaps the difference is sexual. *Photo by:* C. Ferraris.

In these species the dorsal fin does not extend quite as far posteriorly but is still unusually long for catfish. Clariids have broad, flattened heads that usually have large bony plates covering most of the dorsal surface. Four pairs of long barbels, including very prominent nasal barbels, surround the mouths of walking catfish. All species in the family are elongate, some extremely. At least a half dozen species from Africa can be called "eel catfishes" because of the shape of their bodies. Some of these species have pectoral and pelvic fins that are either reduced in size or absent altogether, which further adds to their eel-like appearance.

The "walking" for which this family is named comes about by a combination of characteristics. Although clar-

111

The normal coloration of the walking catfish, *Clarias batrachus,* is seen here. Only rarely is this seen by hobbyists, who are more likely to see albinos. *Photo by:* H. J. Günther.

A fully grown albino walking catfish. *Photo by:* H. J. Günther.

iids lack a dorsal fin spine, the pectoral spines are well developed, and it is on these that the fish propel themselves across land. Breathing during these cross-country forays is accomplished by an accessory structure in the gill cavity that extracts oxygen from the atmosphere, while the delicate gill membranes are kept moist by tightly closed opercles. Thus, clariids are one of several groups of catfishes that are capable of aerial respiration and may actually require access to the atmosphere to survive.

Clariids are quite tolerant of poor water conditions and can survive in a wide range of aquarium conditions. Their air-breathing abilities allow them to live in waters almost devoid of oxygen. Land travel may be more in response to lack of food than to poor water quality, but that has yet to be tested thoroughly. Most species get quite large, though, and are suitable only for large private aquaria or, more often, public viewing.

Clariids are also tolerant of a wide variety of foods. Most are strict carnivores in nature, feeding on both fish and aquatic invertebrates. In the aquarium they often can be trained to accept prepared foods, if training is started early. Those fed on goldfish early can be quite stubborn about maintaining that diet and train their keepers to see their point of view.

Captive reproduction of *Clarias* is of great interest in much of Southeast Asia and Africa, where these fishes are an important food item. Several species have been reported to spawn in ponds, constructing nests in the shallows. *C. batrachus* has also spawned in an aquarium. It is not stated how much parental care is given to the young, but the parents guarded the nest and the eggs immediately after depositing them.

Clariids were always unusual members of the American aquarium market, and only one species, *C. batrachus,* was seen with any regularity. The albino form of this species was kept as a pet or novelty fish, as it does quite well in captivity and grows to well over a foot in length. Other species in the family seemed to be available primarily as contaminants of African shipments.

But all that has changed. The U.S. Fish and Wildlife Service has declared all members of the family Clariidae to be "injurious wildlife" and banned them from this country. It is now illegal to import, transport, or acquire any species of the family without a permit issued by the director of the Fish and Wildlife Service. Such permits are said to be obtainable only for scientific or educational purposes. Thus, clariids are not readily to be found in the American aquarium hobby. However, they still are imported occasionally as contaminants of African and Asian shipments. Those I have seen have been small specimens of the genus *Clarias* and not the albino form, which would stand out too much to slip past the watchful eyes of most exporters.

Doradidae

(*door ADD id dee*)

One of the most popular species of aquarium catfishes, the striped raphael (*Platydoras costatus*), is a member of the family Doradidae, and yet doradids are among the most poorly known and underrepresented catfish families in the hobby. This neglect will, with luck, end someday, bringing doradids to the prominence they deserve.

The family Doradidae, or talking cats, consists of eighty to one hundred species of South American catfish. The name "talking cats" comes from the ability of individuals of many species to make a very audible sound when removed from the water. This sound production is certainly not unique to members of this family, but doradids are among the most "talkative" catfishes, and their name is well deserved.

Platydoras costatus, the striped raphael, is an attractive and peaceful catfish that deserves its popularity. *Photo by:* P. Loiselle.

Doradids often are placed with loricariids and callichthyids as armored cats because of the row of bony plates invariably found along the sides of the body. The resemblance to the true armored cats, though, is only superficial, and doradids are more closely related to a group of naked-skinned catfishes that includes the wood cats and their relatives. The single row of plates, or scutes, that runs along the sides of doradids is characteristic of the group, and that alone is sufficient to place a catfish in this family. These plates run in nearly a straight line from just behind the head to the base of the caudal fin. Each plate has at least one posteriorly directed hook that, together with the other hooks, forms a razor-sharp cutting edge along the side of the fish's body. In many species the plates extend over much of the side of the fish, providing a bony armor. In some species of doradids, however, the plates are small and readily noticeable only just anterior to the caudal fin. Because of this, several species were thought for a while not to belong to this family. In addition to the plates, doradids have several charac-

Even at 2 inches long this *Megalodoras irwini* has well-developed body scutes. *Photo by:* J. O'Malley.

teristics that help to identify them with this family. The dorsal and pectoral spines are always prominent and sturdy. An adipose dorsal fin is always present, though it is never very large and in some species is so tiny that seeing it requires a close examination. The mouth is surrounded by three pairs of barbels, some of which may

Doras punctatus and many other doradids of the sierra catfish group tend to have relatively small lateral scutes that cover only a small fraction of the body's surface. *Photo by:* P. Loiselle.

The branched barbels of this *Opsodoras* are quite well developed. *Photo by:* P. Loiselle.

Acanthodoras cataphractus, the red-striped raphael, is among the most heavily armored of the doradid catfishes. Virtually its entire body is enclosed in plates. *Photo by:* K. Frickhinger.

be branched (or feathery, as it is often referred to in the hobby). A nasal barbel is never present.

With more than thirty genera in the family, identifying species to a genus is somewhat difficult. Doradid genera do divide into two groups, however, based on the shape of their head. One group is recognizable by having a head that is wider than it is high. These depressed-headed doradids almost always have unbranched barbels and a comparatively short snout. This group may justifiably be called the "raphael cats," as they include such well-known species as the striped raphael (*Platydoras costatus*), the spotted raphael (*Agamyxis pectinifrons*), the red-striped raphael (*Acanthodoras cataphractus*), the large snail-eating catfish (*Megalodoras irwini*), and several species of the genus *Amblydoras.* The second group of doradids consists of species in which the head is higher than it is wide, giving the fish a compressed look. Quite often the species in this group have elongated

Pterodoras angeli, from the
Orinoco River system of northern
South America, is occasionally
available in the aquarium hobby.
Photo by: J. O'Malley.

One of the largest of the sierra
cats, *Doras carinatus,* comes from
Guyana and eastern Venezuela.
Photo by: C. Ferraris.

117

snouts with a cluster of feathery barbels at the tip and few if any teeth in their jaws. The barbels are connected by a fleshy membrane, and when the maxillary barbels are pushed forward, all of the barbels are pulled down with the membrane to form an inverted cup. This structure is thrust into the surface of a sandy substrate, and sand and anything contained therein is taken into the mouth. There, the edibles are strained and the unwanted sand is ejected from the oral cavity past the gills and out past the operculum. Thus, the compressed-headed doradids may be thought of as the vacuum cleaners of South American waters. Included in this group are quite a number of species that are seen only

The elongated snout and large head of this sierra cat allow it to vacuum up large quantities of fine sand and sift out the hidden invertebrates that form the bulk of its food. *Photo by:* C. Ferraris.

rarely in the aquarium hobby. When found, they may be sold under the names "sierra cat," "mouse cat," "zipper cat," and, occasionally, "hassar cat." In the following discussion I will refer to this group by the name "sierra cat," or "sierras" for short. To my knowledge, none of these names refers specifically to one species; instead, they are used interchangeably for several of these rarely seen forms. I assume this will change when one or more species in this group are imported with a certain amount of regularity, at which time a name will become more firmly attached to it.

The diversity of doradid species is readily reflected in the size that some of these species achieve. The smallest species, *Physopyxis lyra,* grows to only about ½ inch. In contrast, the dolphin cat (*Pseudodoras niger*), a species that a friend of mine has named the "gentle giant" for its most pleasant demeanor, has been re-

Unlike most doradid catfishes, *Lithodoras dorsalis* has large plates on the dorsal surface of the body in addition to lateral plates. *Photo by:* P. Loiselle.

ported to reach more than 4 feet in length and weigh nearly 45 pounds. But the giants of the Doradidae are rare; most species can be accommodated readily in home aquaria.

Aquarium maintenance of many species in this family is not a problem. Many species of raphael cats are common members of community tanks and seem to thrive in this setting. With the exception of the smallest tetras or rasboras, raphaels seem not to bother tankmates and are tolerant of a wide variety of conditions so long as they are provided with some amount of shelter in which to hide. Their tolerance of other doradids is well known and is often demonstrated by examining a piece of PVC tubing in a community tank. If it is an appropriate size, the tubing will quite likely be stuffed end to end with doradids that seem perfectly content to share the space with members of their species and others. As with water conditions, food is often not

a problem for raphaels. Most accept prepared food so long as it reaches the bottom of the tank. Sierra cats may require a bit more attention to their environment, however. Most sierras live in soft-bottom environments, with either muddy or sandy bases that they can vacuum up to extract whatever food is trapped within. Coarser gravel substrates are too difficult for most of the smaller individuals to take into their buccal cavity, so they are unable to feed normally. Thus, sierras are more properly placed in aquaria (either community or separate) that are fitted with fine sand substrates.

Sierras also differ from raphaels by the manner in which they avoid light. In nature, raphaels hide in rockwork crevices or hollowed-out logs during

The long-nosed raphael, *Orinocodoras eigenmanni,* occasionally can be found in among striped raphaels. *Photo by:* J. O'Malley.

daylight. Sierras, on the other hand, descend into deeper pools in rivers, avoiding the lighted shorelines, and migrate into shallower areas at night to feed. In aquaria it is not possible to provide sierras with a similar environment, but it is essential to provide them with a very dimly lit area into which they can retreat. This can be done with vegetation or creative rockwork, or a combination of both. Finally, unlike raphaels, sierras are gregarious catfishes. In several places in Venezuela I have observed aggregations of literally hundreds of them feeding together along sandy beaches after dark. Thus, I would always consider keeping several of these fishes together, rather than a single specimen or even a pair.

Surprisingly little is known about reproduction in the entire doradid family.

Somewhat over 150 years ago the nest and parental behavior of *Amblydoras hancocki* was described from observations in nature. It was noted that the nest was constructed of leaves, in which a cluster of eggs was placed. The nest and eggs were guarded by the parents at least until the eggs hatched. Since that time almost nothing new has been added to our knowledge of the reproductive biology of this species or the family. Surely this will change when aquarists intent on inducing the spawning of these attractive catfishes begin to succeed.

Heteropneustidae
(*hetter op NOOSE tid dee*)

The Asian family Heteropneustidae is composed of two species of elongated graceful catfishes, one of which, *Heteropneustes fossilis,* the fossil cat, is a well-known aquarium fish. Unfortunately, it seems to be best known for its ability to deliver a potent sting, which is reported to be strong enough to seriously injure or even kill a person; this has justified another common name for this fish: "stinging cat."

Heteropneustids can readily be identified by a combination of structures. The elongated body is strongly compressed, giving the fish a straplike appearance. The anal fin extends for nearly half the length of the body. In contrast, the dorsal fin is small, lacks a spine, and sits just above the equally small pelvic fins. The caudal fin of these fishes is broadly rounded, and an adipose dorsal fin is absent. The mouth of *Heteropneustes* is surrounded by eight barbels, all about the same length and all pointed forward. Only the walking catfishes (family Clariidae) and some Australian catfishes (family Plotosidae) might be confused with these fishes. Clariids, however, have elongated dorsal fins that cover almost the entire dorsal surface of the body; plotosids all have a strong spine at the anterior margin of

the dorsal fin and are generally more robust than *Heteropneustes*.

Heteropneustes is one of several groups of catfishes that have accessory breathing structures, allowing them to obtain needed oxygen directly from the atmosphere. These fishes can gulp air from the surface of the water when there is insufficient oxygen in the water. Even in aquarium situations you may see these fishes periodically coming to the surface for a brief period, sticking their snouts above the water, and returning to the bottom of the tank.

In captivity *H. fossilis* grows to more than a foot in length, but it is usually obtained at a much smaller size. These fishes generally do quite well in captivity and grow quickly. Because of this, they will need to be transferred to

The stinging, or fossil, catfish (*Heteropneustes fossilis*) must be handled with a great deal of care to avoid being stung by one of its venomous pectoral spines. *Photo by:* J. O'Malley.

a larger aquarium as they grow. It is in such transfers that the stinging catfish is most dangerous. Moving one of these fishes without appropriate caution can cause a very painful sting, even from a very small fish.

Maintenance of stinging cats is not difficult. They tolerate a wide range of aquarium conditions and seem to thrive on a variety of foods. Shelter is a must, as it is with most catfishes. They can be placed in community aquaria, but they will freely consume small tankmates, so careful judgment of the size of tankmates is cautioned.

There are reports of aquarium spawnings of *Heteropneustes*. Fishes

Amieurus nebulosus, the brown bullhead, is not very well known among American aquarists, but it is kept by European catfish enthusiasts. *Photo by:* H. Reinhard.

mature at lengths of 8 to 10 inches, but even when mature, there is little sexual dimorphism. Nests are excavated from the substrate, and nest, eggs, and afterward the young are guarded by the parents. Although this fish is larger than most aquarium-spawned species, it is certainly of a size that an interested aquarist could spawn to observe its reproductive behavior.

Ictaluridae
(*ik tah LUHR id dee*)

The freshwaters of North America are home to only one family of catfishes, the Ictaluridae, a group of about forty-five species. Ictalurids are naturally widespread throughout the North American continent east of the Rock-

Young individuals of the albino channel catfish, *Ictalurus punc tatus,* can be found routinely in pet shops and are quite attractive at this small size. *Photo by:* P. Loiselle.

ies, from southern Canada to Guatemala. At present, most of the larger species of the family, belonging to the genera *Ictalurus* and *Amieurus,* have breeding populations in the western states, and in past years a few species were introduced widely into Europe, where they are now the dominant catfishes of that continent.

Species of the family Ictaluridae are diverse in body form and sometimes difficult to distinguish from some other catfishes, especially members of the Afro-Asian family Bagridae. In general, ictalurids can be recognized as being naked-skinned catfishes with four pairs of barbels (the nasal barbels are usually quite prominent) and sturdy spines on the pectoral and dorsal fins. The pelvic fins of ictalurids are unusual in that they have more than six rays, but this is often difficult to recognize in living fishes. Ictalurids are often divided into three major groups: catfishes, bullheads, and the smaller species madtoms, or stonecats. Four other species, the flathead catfish and

three blind cave forms, complete the family. The catfish group, referred to as the genus *Ictalurus,* consists of nine species that can be recognized by a forked caudal fin and an adipose dorsal fin that is substantially smaller than the anal fin. *Ictalurus* species tend to be more free-swimming than the other species of the family, and the tail region is more streamlined. Included in this group is the channel catfish, a common aquarium species, especially as an albino strain. Bullheads are similar in general body shape to *Ictalurus* and are often included in that genus, but they belong to a distinct lineage in the family and deserve a separate generic name. When used, the name *Amieurus* refers to only the bullheads. They are more bottom-oriented than the *Ictalurus* species and

123

It is important to remember that channel catfish can grow to more than 4 feet in length before adding one to a small community aquarium. *Photo by:* P. Loiselle.

seldom swim much above the substrate. They generally have thicker bodies with broader tail regions. In addition, bullheads have emarginate, or squared-off, caudal fins instead of the forked fins of the catfishes. Bullheads are common pond and lake fishes, and young ones can be caught easily with only a small net. Because of this, bullheads are often among the first catfishes that are kept by children.

Madtoms constitute the third and largest group of ictalurid catfish. Unlike the two previous groups, madtoms are quite small, rarely reaching more than 5 inches in length. Most species are even smaller than that, and some reach a maximum of less than 2 inches. Madtoms are usually placed in the genus *Noturus,* but the genus is sometimes split into several smaller groups. These fishes differ from *Ic-*

talurus and *Amieurus* in having an elongated adipose dorsal fin that is as long as the anal fin and is sometimes connected to the caudal fin. In addition, the caudal fin is usually rounded instead of forked or squared off.

Madtoms are usually found in stream riffles, but some species are known from the margins of large lakes. They often live in stony stream beds or stone-laden shores of large lakes, and species differ markedly in their habitat preferences. That they are so commonly found among stones in river bottoms led to the other common name for these fishes, "stonecats."

Ictalurids are quite suitable for aquarium keeping, but almost all species have been overlooked by the hobby, with the exception of a very few dedicated "native fish" aquarists. There are quite a number of attractive species of madtoms that would make most interesting additions to the fish room of a serious catfish hobbyist.

Because they have been kept so infrequently in aquaria, little has been written on them in hobbyist publications. Aquarium spawning of these fishes is virtually unknown, even though at least one species, the channel catfish, is routinely bred in ponds and is a very important commercial species in the southern United States. Although there is a dearth of hobbyist literature on ictalurids, scientific literature about the reproductive biology of these fishes far exceeds that for any other catfish family. In general, ictalurids are known to spawn in nests that are tended by one or both parents. Nest tending extends from before spawning until the young have grown sufficiently large to leave the nesting site. During this period the parent or parents are said to be very attentive to the offspring, constantly guarding them. As any child (or former child) who has observed young bullheads in a pond knows, a keen eye will almost always spot the wary bullhead parent not far from the young—far enough away to be safe from humans, but as close to its offspring as possible.

The strong parental attention of bullheads is probably reflected in the more aquarium-sized madtoms. For this reason alone, madtoms should be part of any catfish hobbyist's fish room. A word of caution, though: although most madtom species are quite abundant in nature, some are rare and protected in some states. All states have wildlife laws regulating the capture of fishes, even nongame or nonfood fishes. Usually catfishes can be taken with dip nets or small seines, provided that a valid fishing license has been obtained. So before going out in search of madtoms, be sure to check with the appropriate fish and game officials for the rules that apply to that state.

The slender madtom, *Noturus exilis*, is among the many small North American catfishes that remain unknown to American fish enthusiasts. *Photo by:* P. Loiselle.

Loricariidae

(*lohr ih care EE id dee*)

The family Loricariidae is by far the largest family of catfishes. More than 450 species are recognized at present, and several more are named every year. Loricariids are generally known in the aquarium hobby as "suckermouthed cats," "armored cats," or, better, "armored suckermouth cats," due to the two traits that most easily distinguish them from other catfishes.

Loricariids can be recognized by the overlapping plates of bone covering most if not all of their bodies and by the ventrally directed, suckerlike mouth, which usually has a large, fleshy lower lip. Beyond these two characteristics, the diversity of form in

The gold-trimmed pleco is only one of the many attractive loricariids that have appeared in the hobby recently. *Photo by:* P. Loiselle.

this family is so overwhelming that it defies simple generalization.

Aquarists usually recognize three groups of loricariids. The most widely known is the plecostomus group, which gets its name from an old but scientifically unacceptable name for these fishes. The plecos, as they are generally called, include fish that have a comparatively large head with a broad snout and a caudal area that is cylindrical or conical (but not flattened). Usually members of the pleco group have an adipose fin, although some species do not. Among the best-known members of the pleco group are the common plecos (genus *Hypostomus*), long-finned plecos (*Pterygoplichthys*), bristle nose plecos (*Ancistrus*), panaques (*Panaque*), and clown plecos (*Peckoltia*). These groups have long been in the aquarium hobby and are becoming more popular every day.

The second group is commonly referred to as the "whiptailed cats." Whiptails have a more slender body

This species of *Chaetostoma* is pigmented in such a way that the rows of overlapping plates can be seen quite easily. *Photo by:* P. Loiselle.

than plecos, and, as can be guessed from the name, the tail region is long, slender, and flattened, so that the tail is much wider than it is deep. Often one or more of the caudal fin rays is prolonged into a slender filament, which may extend beyond the tail for a distance equal to the length of the entire body of the fish. Unlike the plecos, whiptails never have an adipose dorsal fin. One of the best-known whiptails, the stick cat (genus *Farlowella*), has to be considered one of the most unusual members of the group. The elongated body that characterizes the group is carried to an extreme in these fishes. A foot-long individual may have a body no thicker than a pencil and a snout that is prolonged to a slender tip. More typical of the whiptail group are the genera *Rineloricaria* and *Sturisoma,* which are sold either as whiptails or as loricaria and royal farlowella, and are seen occasionally in the hobby.

The third group of loricariids familiar to fish keepers is the otocinclus group.

Although all loricariids have suckermouths full of teeth, species of *Chaetostoma* take the prize for the widest, most toothy mouths of the family. *Photo by:* P. Loiselle.

127

Pseudacanthicus spinosus can best be distinguished from other armored suckermouth catfishes by the large spines that ornament its dermal scutes. *Photo by:* P. Loiselle.

At present, any pleco that has a large, many-rayed dorsal fin is usually placed in the genus *Pterygoplichthys*. *Photo by:* P. Loiselle.

The well-known blue-eyed pleco, *Panaque suttoni,* is the most commonly available species of a genus that includes many attractive species. *Photo by:* J. O'Malley.

While the two other groups in the family contain both large and small species, all members of the otocinclus group are quite small and readily lend themselves to even the smallest of aquaria. The two genera of the otocinclus group found in the aquarium hobby are readily distinguished from other loricariids by their eyes. Species of *Otocinclus* and *Hypoptopoma* have large eyes located on the lateral margins of the head. The eyes can be seen from beneath the fish when, for example, it is resting on the front glass of an aquarium. In other loricariids the eyes are located dorsally on the head, and the eyes cannot be seen from below.

The early popularity of loricariids seems to be related to their propensity for eating algae. Plecos were bought as worker fishes to clean the walls and rockwork of aquaria, with little other interest in the fish. But that seems to be changing somewhat now, especially as more attractive species of armored suckermouth cats are becom-

ing more readily available. The generally mellow personality of many of these catfishes is attracting more aquarists, who keep loricariids as equal members of community aquaria or as special fish in tanks of their own. Recently the conditions necessary to encourage loricariids to spawn became better known, and these fishes have now joined *Corydoras* as the most popular catfish in breeding tanks. Now virtually every issue of European and American aquarium hobby magazines announces the discovery or spawning of yet another species of loricariid.

Maintaining loricariids in aquaria is generally not a problem, but introducing them into aquaria sometimes is (see under "Adding Catfish to Existing Aquaria" in the chapter "The Catfish

129

Species of the genus *Peckoltia*, such as this *P. pulcher*, lend themselves to small community aquaria because of their own diminutive size. *Photo by:* M. Smith.

Aquarium"). Many loricariids are partial to fast-flowing water and sensitive to water quality. These fishes will often show signs of stress long before most other catfishes are affected by the buildup of nitrogenous wastes in the water. For these species, power filters or under-gravel filters with power heads provide the desired water movement, and frequent water changes keep the nitrogen buildup under control. One notable exception to this are the royal farlowellas, *Sturisoma* spp., which seem to react

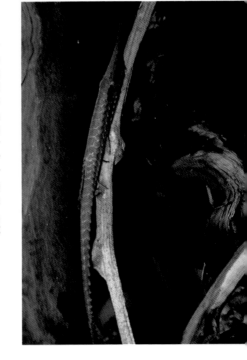

The stick catfishes of the genus *Farlowella* live in swift-flowing streams and rivers and seem to do well in captivity only when fast-moving water is incorporated into the aquarium. *Photo by:* H. Sosna.

Although the head of a *Farlowella* may not look very much like that of other loricariids, the ventral surface shows the typical suckermouth that characterizes this family. *Photo by:* H. Sosna.

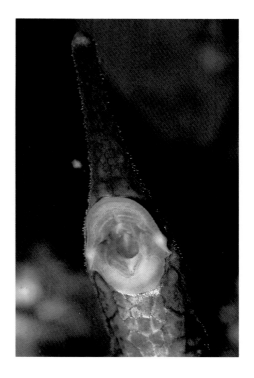

quite badly to great changes in their water; they may quickly go into stress, and often die. For these species, frequent small changes are appropriate.

Nearly all loricariids are herbivores, and, like most herbivores, they require large amounts of plant matter to sustain themselves. Unlike most other catfishes, loricariids are active in the day, and they also spend a large amount of their time feeding. Thus, feeding loricariids requires a strategy that differs from the one used for other

Royal farlowella (species of the genus *Sturisoma*) are characterized by the falcate, or sickle-shaped, dorsal fin. *Photo by:* H. Sosna.

131

In contrast to the commonly available *Otocinclus*, species of the rarely available genus *Parotocinclus* have small, dorsolaterally placed eyes and a prominent adipose fin. *Photo by:* M. Smith.

Otocinclus species are quite often available in the aquarium hobby. Note the large laterally placed eyes and the absence of an adipose fin: two characteristics that help identify members of this genus. *Photo by:* M. Smith.

While most species of armored suckermouth catfish thrive on algae and other vegetable matter, some species, such as the newly discovered vampire pleco, may eat invertebrates. *Photo by:* P. Loiselle.

A close-up of the mouth of the vampire pleco showing the elongated teeth in the upper and lower jaws clustered near the middle of the mouth. *Photo by:* P. Loiselle.

catfishes. Food should be made available at all times so that the fishes can feed as needed, rather than getting a daily quantity to be consumed at one time. Finally, it appears that all loricariids require some amount of wood in their diet. Perhaps it is used as roughage, just as humans use plant matter, but there is evidence that some of the most aggressive wood eaters, the panaques, actually digest the wood as an important part of their nutritional intake. Because of this, it is essential to have some amount of sunken driftwood in an aquarium containing armored suckermouth cats. In this same vein, it should be noted that very often loricariids seem to use driftwood as a place to hang out as well as feed. If a goal of an individual aquarium is to

133

One of several interesting species of the genus *Panaque,* currently going by the name watermelon pleco. It has not yet been given a scientific name. *Photo by:* P. Loiselle.

house two or more similar species of loricariids, it may be wise to include enough pieces of wood spaced throughout the aquarium so that each catfish can have access to it without first having to oust another fish from its claimed piece, thereby eliminating one

A piece of driftwood is often the focal point of activity for loricariid catfishes. *Photo by:* C. Ferraris.

The genus *Parancistrus*, with its one species (*P. auranticus*), is distinguished from other suckermouths in that its dorsal fin and adipose fin are connected by a membrane. *Photo by:* P. Loiselle.

Although the elongated *Isorineloricaria spinosissimus* (which sometimes goes by the name *I. festae*) looks quite a bit like a whiptail catfish, the presence of an adipose fin is a clear indication that it is actually a long-bodied pleco. *Photo by:* P. Loiselle.

Males of all species of the genus *Ancistrus* develop cephalic tentacles along the margin of the snout and between the eyes. *Photo by:* P. Loiselle.

The length, position, and degree of branching of cephalic tentacles can be used to help in the identification of various species of *Ancistrus*. *Photo by:* P. Loiselle.

source of conflict from the tank. Panaques are so demanding about having wood to chew on that they will chew on other aquarium parts if wood is unavailable. Such notoriously non-nutritious substances as filter uptake tubes and aquarium glass sealer have

succumbed to panaque appetites, with obvious disastrous consequences to both the aquarium and the fish (not to mention the carpeting!). Although we are still just beginning to learn about the biology of armored suckermouth cat reproduction, what has been learned already is quite enough to conclude that this family has as diverse a repertoire of behaviors as it does forms. Sexual dimorphism is evident in a large proportion of species in the family. Sometimes the dimorphism is exhibited by the presence of enlarged odontodes scattered over the body or concentrated in one place. Male zucchini cats (*Isorineloricaria spinossissimus*), for example, are densely covered with fine spinelike odontodes over most of their body. In addition, larger and thicker odontodes can be found on the upper surface of their pectoral spines. During reproductive season these odontodes make the distinction between males and females quite obvious. For the remainder of the year the

Many species of loricariids deposit eggs in burrows built in the banks of rivers and ponds. On the bank of the Ucayali River of Peru, burrows at different elevations suggest that the river is home to quite a number of species of suckermouthed catfishes. *Photo by:* C. Ferraris.

differences between the sexes is much less obvious and in some species almost impossible to detect. Many species of the pleco group show similar kinds of seasonal odontode growth in males. Also, the well-known bristle nose catfishes (*Ancistrus* species) show yet another kind of sexual dimorphism on their snouts. Soft, fleshy tentacles appear on the middle of the snout and along the front margin of the head. The largest tentacles are often branched at least once, giving the snout a bushy appearance. Unfortunately, the name "bristle nose catfish" was given to these fishes early on in the history of the hobby. The appendages on the snout are anything but bristly; they appear more like the tentacles of a sea anemone. The tentacles can be found in both sexes of most species of the genus, but they are invariably larger in males. Many whiptails show similar increases in odontode development, usually on the head and pectoral fins. The sides of the head of breeding males often appear to have patches of Velcro beneath the eyes, due to the heavy concentration of small odontodes.

At this time reproductive biology is known for only a small fraction of the armored suckermouths. Within the pleco group, the larger sailfin and common plecos deposit their eggs in caves excavated in mudbanks along the edges of rivers or even farm ponds. In periods of low water that correspond to the dry season, the openings of these now-vacant caves

can be seen to form vertical catfish condos along the exposed banks. Different sizes and heights of the openings suggest that several different species use the same bank but spawn at different times, as the water level changes.

While caves in mudbanks seem to play an important role in the reproduction of larger pleco species, the smaller bristle noses are content with much more modest shelters. In aquaria, bristle noses can often be bred in a tank containing only a single flower pot shard or a length of PVC tubing. In both of these groups, as in all armored suckermouths, the male guards the spawn vigorously until the young fish hatch. Thereafter, the parents seem to have no role in the lives of the young, which are left to fend for themselves immediately.

Unlike plecos, some whiptails spawn in the open and not in caves. Royal farlowellas place their eggs on vertical surfaces such as the walls of an aquarium, which can make obser-

Royal farlowellas place their spawn on vertical surfaces, such as the walls of an aquarium. The male guards the eggs until they hatch. *Photo by:* J. Mancusi.

vations on the developing embryos quite easy. Males of a couple of genera of whips (including *Loricariichthys* and *Pseudohemiodon,* neither of which is regularly imported yet in the aquarium hobby) guard their eggs in a most unusual manner. Instead of being placed in one spot and protected, the plaque of eggs is glued to the lower surface of the male's fleshy lower lip and carried around for the entire length of their development. Should the male be disturbed, the eggs can be dislodged from their place (and most likely eaten by other fishes). I am not certain whether such an egg mass would survive under aquarium conditions in the absence of egg predators.

As more species of armored suckermouths are imported and kept with the hope of breeding them, I expect that the pages of local and national aquarium journals will be filled with accounts of novel forms of reproductive behavior that are beyond our imagination at this time.

A juvenile *Acanthicus adonis,* one of the most spectacular of the recently imported armored suckermouth catfishes. *Photo by:* M. Smith.

Malapteruridae
(*mahl lap tur RUHR id dee*)

The African electric catfish family Malapteruridae is among the best-known of all catfishes. Electric catfishes are exhibited in many public aquaria and can often be found in pet stores, both for sale and as display animals. The unusual appearance of these catfishes and the mystique that comes with being electric make them a widely sought fish. Despite this, very little is known about them, especially in nature.

The family Malapteruridae is easily recognized by a number of anatomical features. The body is that of an elongated sausage with barbels and fins. Even the fins are notable, as electric catfishes are the only ones that lack a

An electric catfish, *Malapterurus
electricus. Photo by:* M. Smith.

dorsal fin. Only the adipose dorsal fin
breaks up the smooth dorsal contour
that extends from the tip of the snout
nearly to the caudal fin. The mouth is
surrounded by three pairs of barbels of
approximately equal length. Most individuals are marked with an irregular
series of black spots over much of the
body. The spots may be absent, however, leaving only three more or less
vertical black bars on the tail region
and caudal fin.

There are two recognized species in
the family, both belonging to the
genus *Malapterurus.* The species
commonly seen, *M. electricus,* is
known throughout much of tropical
Africa and is distinguished from the
second species, *M. microstomus,* by
its larger mouth and different number
of vertebrae. Examination of a large
number of specimens imported from
western Africa never revealed any *M.
microstomus,* which suggests that
only *M. electricus* is available to aquarists.

Electric cats are probably best
known for their ability to generate
electricity and administer an electric
shock at will. The nature of the electricity is discussed more fully in the
chapter "Handling Catfishes" and will
not be repeated here. Electric cats use
their electrical ability for more than
shocking unwary aquarists, however.
It is thought to be of primary use as a
way of stunning potential prey that
comes close to the lethargic predatory
catfishes. A long burst of electrical discharge may be sufficient to immobilize
a small fish long enough for the electric cat to maneuver into position and
swallow it. It has been shown recently
that the electrical discharges are also
used as a form of communication
between electric cats and other species of catfishes, occasionally during

fights.

Electric cats grow to more than 3 feet in length and may approach 50 pounds. In the aquarium hobby, fishes of 3 to 5 inches are most commonly available, but with proper care these fishes grow quite quickly. In general, tank conditions are quite flexible, except that a separate tank must be dedicated to a single electric cat; only rarely will they tolerate any other fishes in their aquarium, and the result of their intolerance is usually the death of an intruder. Feeding electric cats is also comparatively easy. They can be fed a wide variety of meaty foods. Feeder goldfish are readily accepted but not necessary. Although other animals are probably preferred (earthworms, krill, and so forth), I suspect that with a little effort electric cats could be trained to accept sinking pelletized food. Shelter is a must for these fishes if the tank is in a lighted location. Like many catfishes, they prefer dimly lighted situations and are most active in the crepuscular light of dawn and dusk.

Electric cats are extremely territorial fishes that must be kept alone in most aquarium situations. For many catfishes, an aquarium that is too small to house more than one territorial individual can often be subdivided artificially to create a number of small territories in which several can reside. This seems not to work very well for electric cats, however, as large individuals have been known to make rounds from shelter to shelter and methodically drive all others out of their resting places. This unwillingness to share limited amounts of space makes aquarium spawning a distinctly difficult operation. To my knowledge, no one has yet observed spawning in these fishes, and the conditions necessary

Synodontis multipunctatus from Lake Tanganyika. *Photo by:* B. Kahl.

to stimulate reproductive activities are unknown. Even in the field, almost nothing is known about the environmental conditions that can be found during the reproductive season of these fishes.

Electric cats must be placed in the category of "not for everyone." They grow large and require an aquarium of their own. In addition, by law they may not be kept in the state of Florida. Breeding them will require an extra effort to learn the secrets both of keeping two fishes together and of finding the right conditions for spawning. But, aside from this, they are clearly a novelty that deserves notice. They are not very demanding about living conditions or food, and they can make an interesting pet fish or an addition to the fish room of many dedicated catfish keepers.

It is occasionally possible to find the diminutive *Mochokiella paynei* in shipments of West African fishes. *Photo by:* P. Loiselle.

Mochokidae
(*moh COKE id dee*)

The African catfish family Mochokidae is best known among hobbyists as the group that includes the upside-down catfish and its relatives, known collectively as "Synodontis cats" or "squeakers." *Synodontis* includes many attractive species that often lend themselves quite well to aquarium conditions. As a group *Synodontis* is, after *Corydoras,* among the most widely kept and sought-after catfishes for the aquarium.

The family Mochokidae is one of several in which the nuchal region (the area between the back of the head and the origin of the dorsal fin) is covered with a plate of heavy bone, which contributes to a continuous bony shield from behind the eyes to the dorsal fin spine. The South American families Doradidae, Auchenipteridae, and Centromochlidae all possess this same bony plate. Mochokids differ

from these other families by having a ventrally placed or downturned mouth, which sometimes looks very similar to that in the armored suckermouth catfishes of the family Loricariidae. Several other characteristics also help to distinguish mochokids from other catfishes. Nasal barbels are always absent, and both pairs of mental barbels are usually branched or feathered. An adipose dorsal fin is always present and quite often large and fleshy. In general appearance, many species, especially those of the genus *Synodontis*, look similar to species of the family Doradidae, but no species of mochokid has the plates on the side of the body that so readily characterize doradids.

The nearly 150 species of the family can be divided into two groups. The first includes those species with a more or less normal catfish head, which contains the speciose genus *Synodontis*, the diminutive *Mochokiella paynei*, and a few other genera that rarely if ever are imported as

The characteristic color pattern and sparsely branched mental barbels help to identify *Mochokiella. Photo by:* P. Loiselle.

Most species of *Synodontis* have extensively branched mental barbels, as seen in this *S. eupterus. Photo by:* P. Loiselle.

Another view of *Synodontis eupterus. Photo by:* P. Loiselle.

aquarium fishes. The second group contains the suckermouth mochokids, all of which have a broad, ventrally oriented mouth with rows of teeth on an enlarged plate on the upper jaw. This peculiar arrangement of upper jaw teeth allows these fishes to scrape food off rocky substrates. About fifty species make up this group, which consists of three genera: *Chiloglanis, Euchilichthys,* and *Atopochilus.* Only rarely are any of these fishes imported into the American market, but they do find their way into European aquaria at times.

Keeping *Synodontis* and its relatives can be quite easy. Most species are nocturnal and prefer dim light, even in the day. If the aquarium is well lit, a number of hiding places should be available. Most species are reasonably peaceful toward other species and can therefore be added to community aquaria. In contrast, healthy individuals are often intolerant of con-specifics and will relentlessly harass others in the same aquarium. While many species can be kept in home aquaria, a few grow to sizes that exceed 2 feet in length and are therefore suitable only for public display. Many of the available species are tolerant of a broad range of conditions and can be fed on a wide variety of foods, both live and prepared. Species coming from the African great lakes (for example, *S. multipunctatus, S. petricola, S. nijassae,* and the rare but elegant *S. granulosus*) are from hard alkaline waters and should be kept, at least initially, in similar conditions. Most other species will do well in more neutral or even slightly acidic water.

The suckermouth mochokids must be viewed quite differently. These species are primarily algae-eating fishes, similar to loricariids. They have more restricted dietary preferences, which must be catered to for their health. Algae must be provided in abundance or a suitable substitute found. Armored suckermouth catfish keepers have provided their fish with a diet of zucchini or spinach leaves with great success (see under "Food" in the chapter "The Catfish Aquarium"). Presumably this same approach could be used for mochokids. In addition, suckermouths are often found in swift-moving waters, such as rapids. Accessories that move water in aquaria, such as power heads on under-gravel systems or power filters, can be used to create a flow of water over the surface of a large piece of driftwood or slate, to simulate an environment similar to the one from which these fishes come.

Although widely kept by hobbyists, mochokids, and especially species of *Synodontis,* have not been particularly forthcoming about their spawning requirements. Only a very few reports of aquarium spawning have been published. The commonly available species *S. nigriventris,* the upside-down cat, has been observed to spawn in aquaria, as have a few other species. Eggs are either deposited in clusters in a secluded or protected area or are scattered around as the spawning fish swim over the substrate. In either case, no nest construction was noticed, nor was guarding of the eggs observed. Although relatively little is known about reproductive activities in squeakers, one of the most unusual forms of reproduction in catfishes is known from this family. The Lake Tanganyika endemic, *S. multipunctatus,* exhibits the only case of brood parasitism known in catfishes. As described in detail in the chapter "Reproduction," the multipuncs pawn off their spawn onto oral-brooding cichlids, which seem to care for them as well as they do their own offspring. With the great variety of forms and native habitat from which mochokids come, one can only begin to guess what other interesting behaviors these fishes may exhibit in their reproductive activities.

At first glance *Synodontis petricola* is sometimes mistaken for another Lake Tanganyika species, *S. multipunctatus. Photo by:* J. O'Malley.

Synodontis angelicus is among the best-known species of the family Mochokidae. For years it was among the most sought-after and expensive catfish in the hobby. *Photo by:* P. Loiselle.

Synodontis decorus, one of the more striking species of that genus. *Photo by:* P. Loiselle.

Pangasiidae
(*pan gas IE id dee*)

The family Pangasiidae forms a small group of South and Southeast Asian catfishes. Most if not all of the two dozen species in the family are free-swimming, midwater fishes that move in schools, at least when small.

Pangasiids are characterized by a sleek, graceful body that seems to glide effortlessly through the water. Quite often these fishes have eyes that are unusually large for catfishes, a characteristic that is often useful in recognizing them. The best characteristic for identification, however, is one that takes a practiced eye to spot: pangasiids have only one set of barbels on their chin. That pair and the ever-present maxillary barbels are the only ones to be found in species of this family. So if more than two pairs of barbels are seen, it's not a pangasiid!

Were it not for the iridescent shark (*Pangasius sutchi*), the family Pangasiidae would be virtually unknown to aquarists. Because of this one species, however, the family is quite well known in most hobbyist circles. Inch-long iridescent sharks are among the most eye-catching of fishes, and they often can be found in even small community aquaria. Unfortunately, their eye-catching beauty and the frenetic swimming behavior of a tankful of these fishes in a pet shop aquarium are little indication of what the proud owner of one or two of these has to look forward to.

Iridescent sharks are quite clearly schooling fishes, at least when small. They do not seem to be quite so bold or active when not in the company of a half dozen or more conspecifics. That alone is hardly a reason to complain; I personally think schools of catfishes are among the most attractive

The iridescent shark, which currently goes by the name *Pangasius sutchi,* is the only species of the family Pangasiidae that is readily available to hobbyists. *Photo by:* P. Loiselle.

At present U.S. law prohibits the importation or possession of the long-finned pangasius, *Pangasius sanitwongsei. Photo by:* P. Loiselle.

of underwater sights. But iridescent sharks grow incredibly quickly, reaching lengths of a foot or more in a year or two under good conditions. That school of six or eight tiny catfishes can quite quickly outgrow a fifty-five- or hundred-gallon aquarium.

So what starts out as a small school of community aquarium fish can quickly become a roomful of pet fish. As pet fish, iridescent sharks are most acceptable. They seem to respond quite well to humans, especially those with food in hand. But, as with any pet fish, there is a commitment of space and food that should be known and understood *before* undertaking the responsibility.

In the last year or so, a second species of pangasiid has appeared in the hobby sporadically. This most attractive fish looks very similar to the irides-cent shark, but it has longer dorsal and anal fins and is attractively marked with black fins. These fishes are the young of one of the truly giant catfishes, *P. sanitwongsei.* When they first appeared, it was clear they would be a welcome and sought-after addition to the hobby, but that idea was short-lived. Soon after the identity of that fish was established, it was found that the species had been listed as endangered. As such, import into the United States is prohibited. It would appear that the Thais have discovered a way to pond-raise this species, which may eventually lead to its rescue from the brink of extinction. If this is the case, all catfish enthusiasts should take heart, for once the species is safely reestablished, it may be possible to remove the fish from the endangered species list and bring these most attractive catfishes back into the hobby.

Pimelodidae

(*pim meh LOAD id dee*)

The Pimelodidae are the largest group of naked-skinned catfishes in the world. More than 300 species are named, and many additional forms are found each year. Included in the family are some of the largest and smallest species of catfishes, and in my opinion some of the best pet fishes.

Pimelodids are found throughout South and Central America and are often a dominant part of the fauna wherever they are found. The diversity of body forms in this family is so great that it is almost impossible to categorize. Some species of this family look so similar to other naked catfish families, such as the North American Ictaluridae and the Afro-Asian Bagridae, that misidentifications are not uncommon. There are, however, a few characteristics that help in the recognition of pimelodids. All species in this family lack nasal barbels, which distinguishes this family from the ictalurids,

many bagrids, and quite a number of other families of catfishes. In addition, pimelodids generally have very long maxillary barbels, which sometimes exceed the length of the fish itself. Unfortunately, this is not always the case, and some species of pimelodids have remarkably short and indistinct barbels.

Identification of pimelodids is further made difficult by variation in the position of the dorsal fin. As in most catfishes, the dorsal fin is usually found just behind the head. In several pimelodids, however, the fin is located well back, above the middle of the body. And although the dorsal fin spine of many pimelodids is notorious for the painful sting, quite a number of species have no spine at all. Instead, the first ray of the fin is soft and some-

The long, slender barbels that are so evident in this juvenile tiger shovel nose (*Pseudoplatystoma* sp.) are usually found in species of the Neotropical family Pimelodidae. *Photo by:* J. O'Malley.

149

times extended as a long filament.

Almost all pimelodids are voracious predators. Because of this, even the comparatively small and attractive species, such as the angelicus cat, *Pimelodus pictus,* must be added to community aquaria only with larger fishes. The predatory habits of these fishes are a mixed blessing. While they require a bit of extra thought before being added to a community aquarium, they are usually quite easy to feed and care for. Rarely are pimelodids finicky about their food, and when they are, it is usually the result of overpampering by their keeper.

Although species of pimelodid catfish of various sizes are kept by hobbyists, pimelodids are probably best known in the aquarium hobby for the few large species that are often kept as pets. First among these is the South American red-tailed cat, *Phrac-*

Some pimelodids, such as this *Pseudopimelodus raninus,* have quite short maxillary barbels. *Photo by:* P. Loiselle.

tocephalus hemioliopterus. This strikingly marked fish is unmistakable in appearance and is one of the largest species of catfishes to be found. They do quite well in captivity and can grow to quite a large size (although probably not to the 5 feet and 180 pounds plus that they attain in the Amazon). Several other species of pimelodids are equally captivating as pets. The species of sailfin pimelodids, belonging to the genera *Leiarius* and *Perrunichthys,* have become quite popular in recent years. Although they are often imported at the already large size of a foot or more, occasionally sailfins can be found at substantially smaller sizes. Several species of shovel nose pimelodids have also been kept as pets, sometimes with great success. It has been suggested that shovel noses are a bit more difficult to acclimate to aquarium conditions and also to coax into eating prepared foods, so they may not be appropriate candidates for any but the most dedicated catfish keepers.

A strikingly attractive juvenile *Brachyplatystoma juruense*. *Photo by:* P. Loiselle.

As seen in this young *Duo-palatinus*, the maxillary barbel may sometimes exceed the length of the fish. *Photo by:* J. O'Malley.

The striped shovel nose catfish, *Sorubim lima,* is one of only a few shovel nose species that do not grow too large to be kept in an aquarium of 30 gallons or less. *Photo by:* Tetra Archives.

The angelicus catfish, *Pimelodus pictus,* undoubtedly the best-known and most readily available pimelodid, can quickly outstay its welcome in a community aquarium of small fishes because of its voracious feeding habits. *Photo by:* P. Loiselle.

Once available only at lengths of 1 foot or greater, baby South American red-tailed catfishes as small as this 1½-inch individual are now available with increasing frequency. *Photo by:* J. O'Malley.

Sailfin pimelodids, such as this juvenile *Leiarius marmoratus,* also make excellent pet fish and, like the red-tailed catfish, are being imported at very small sizes now. *Photo by:* J. O'Malley.

The purchase of a large pimelodid catfish is a multifaceted commitment, not very different from buying a large dog. Adequate space and a large amount of food must be provided for the ever-growing pet. And because aquaria are almost always on the small side, high-volume filtration systems coupled with frequent water changes are necessary. As with a large furry pet, however, the commitment necessary to keep a large fish is often repaid by attentiveness that is rarely seen in smaller species of catfishes and fishes in general.

Curiously, although pimelodids are among the best-known aquarium catfishes, almost nothing is known about their reproduction. It is understandable that none of the large fishes kept as pets has shown signs of reproductive activity in the aquarium, because most of these fishes are still juveniles, but it is much less understandable why the small species, such as the angelicus cat and the South American bumblebee cats (genus *Microglanis*), have not yet spawned in captivity. This seems to be a most worthy challenge for serious catfish keepers.

Hemisorubim platyrhynchos, the spotted (or porthole) shovel nose catfish, can be readily distinguished from all other shovel noses by its projecting lower jaw. Generally, it is the upper jaw that extends farther forward in these fishes. *Photo by:* J. O'Malley.

At a length of 3 or 4 inches, this young *Paulicea lutkeni* appears to be an attractive addition to a catfish fish room. But it can grow to more than 5 feet in length and over 200 pounds—well beyond the capability of any but a public aquarium. *Photo by:* M. Smith.

Microglanis species, among the smallest pimelodids, are good candidates for hobbyists' efforts toward aquarium breeding. *Photo by:* O. Böhm.

Sexual dimorphism in catfish species may be simply differences in coloration, as appears to be the case in *Microglanis. Photo by:* O. Böhm.

The ever-growing South American red-tailed catfish, *Phractocephalus hemioliopterus,* is a hands-down favorite as a pet fish, provided adequate aquarium space is given to it. *Photo by:* P. Loiselle.

Plotosidae

(*ploh TOE sid dee*)

The plotosids, or eel-tailed cats, are virtually unknown to freshwater aquarists. In contrast, one species of this family, *Plotosus lineatus,* known as the "coral cat," can be found quite commonly in marine aquaria. This strange twist in emphasis is indicative of the perception that these catfishes are generally of marine origin. In fact, the majority of species in this family are freshwater, but because they hail only from Australia and New Guinea, they are rarely seen by aquarists.

Eel-tailed cats can be readily recognized by the peculiar form of their tail. All species have an elongated anal fin that is connected to the caudal fin so that the two appear as one continuous structure. In some species there is a continuation of this caudal-anal fin along the dorsal part of the tail, so that the entire posterior part of the fish is lined with a fin. It is for these species that the name "eel-tailed catfish" is most appropriate, but the name is reasonably well suited to the entire family. In addition to the continuous fin, plotosids can be recognized by their four pairs of barbels surrounding the mouth. Generally the barbels are of approximately equal length, and the mental barbels are located just below the lower lip. The barbels are usually held erect and pointing forward, so that the mouth seems surrounded by a mass of tentacles. An adipose dorsal fin is never present in plotosids, which further helps distinguish them from most other catfishes.

Freshwater species in this family are limited to the rivers of New Guinea and Australia. Marine and estuarine species, on the other hand, are widely distributed throughout the western Pacific and Indian oceans and in the Red Sea. There are about thirty species in the family, and although some of them can be quite abundant, surprisingly little was known about their biology until recently. Most of the freshwater species are of a size that would make them appropriate for home aquaria, and several are quite attractive.

Reproduction has been observed in only one freshwater species, *Tandanus tandanus,* from eastern Australia. One of the largest species in the family, it has been reported to grow to nearly 3 feet in length, and may not be mature until it reaches half that size. Although this species may never become a popular aquarium catfish, the information on its spawning may be helpful to someone trying to spawn one of the smaller species. Courtship seems to be initiated by elevated water temperatures, up to approximately 75 degrees. Males build elevated nests of sand and gravel and constantly patrol above and around them. When ready to spawn, a female approaches the nest, and spawning ensues. Afterward, the female leaves or is chased out of the nest area, and the eggs are guarded and tended by the male.

The commonly seen marine coral cat is an excellent addition to marine aquaria. Young members of this species are readily recognized by their alternating black and white (or yellow) stripes running from head to tail. They are common inhabitants of coral reefs and sandy beach areas, where they are usually seen as tightly balled schools of dozens of fish. Schools take on a nearly spherical shape that has been thought to resemble a single large black sea urchin. As the fish get

In eel-tailed catfish, such as this *Neosilurus* sp., the anal fin and caudal fin are joined together. *Photo by:* H. Hansen.

larger, the schools become smaller and the fishes seem to become more reclusive, hiding under coral heads or other darkened shelters. It is widely recognized among fishermen native to places inhabited by *Plotosus lineatus* that the venomous spines of these fishes are to be taken seriously. In the Philippines, plotosids are routinely caught in beach seines, along with a wide variety of other fishes, including several other venomous species. When eel-tailed cats are part of the catch, a noticeable change overtakes the fishermen. Instead of working as quickly as possible to grab the fishes, the fishermen all stop and wait while one of them goes and carefully removes all the catfishes from the net with the aid of a stick. It is very clear that getting stung by a plotosid is something they want to avoid, if at all possible.

Aquarium spawning of coral cats has recently been accomplished. More than one observation was made of a pair of these saltwater plotosids depositing eggs on the substrate of aquaria that were linked into a centralized filtration system. The water was reported to be "normal" marine water, with 76 degree temperature, 8.1 pH, virtually no ammonia or nitrites, and a nitrate content of 50 parts per million. The spawnings resulted in viable offspring that seemed to take to eating brine shrimp nauplii almost immediately.

Unfortunately, freshwater eel-tailed cats are unlikely ever to become widely available to aquarists outside of Australia. We will have to depend on our colleagues from down under to keep us informed of the newest finds on these interesting catfishes.

Schilbidae

(*SKILL bid dee*)

Schilbids form a little-known family of catfishes that hail from both Africa and Asia. About sixty species are known, but only a few species can be found in the aquarium hobby at present.

Schilbids are hard to characterize because the diversity of forms within the family is quite large. Generally, species of the family have long anal fins, sometimes greater than half the length of the entire body. Most species have the full complement of barbels (four pairs) surrounding the mouth, and often they are all quite long and prominent. Usually the dorsal fin is well developed and a tiny adipose fin can be found. Either or both of these fins may be absent, however, in some species of the family. In many ways species of the family are very similar to members of the Asian family Siluridae, and they can easily be confused. Silurids, however, never have an adipose fin, and the dorsal fin is always quite small. Silurids also lack a nasal barbel.

Many schilbids are midwater swimmers and seem most comfortable in schools. The best-known aquarium-kept members of the family, the debauwi cats (*Eutropiellus debauwi* and *E. buffei*), exhibit this penchant for schooling quite well. As midwater-schooling fishes prefer to be in groups, often the larger the better, it is never a good idea to keep fishes such as debauwi cats in groups of less than six. Lesser-known but equally attractive are several other species of midwater schilbids of the genera *Paralia* and *Physalia*. *Physalia pellucida* is the

Debauwi catfish make excellent additions to community aquaria when added in groups of six or more. *Photo by:* B. Kahl.

159

Unlike the similarly shaped
Siluridae, schilbids (such as this
Eutropius sp.) have nasal barbels
and almost always an adipose fin.
Photo by: P. Loiselle.

The grass cutter, *Schilbe mystus,*
is the schilbid most commonly
available to hobbyists. *Photo by.*
B. Kahl.

African equivalent of the more commonly known glass cats and is readily mistaken for them. Note, however, that *Physalia* has an adipose fin and true glass cats do not.

Not all schilbids are active midwater swimmers, however. The commonly seen grass cutter (*Schilbe mystus*) is more at home on the bottom, and alone.

Keeping members of this catfish family under aquarium conditions appears to be quite easy. The midwater-swimming species readily feed from the surface or in the water column and do not seem to be at all finicky about food. For them, flake foods are both adequate and appropriate. The species that are more commonly found near the aquarium bottom are also very hardy in general. Like the majority of catfishes, they thrive on a variety of live foods but can readily be trained to eat sinking pellets.

Little has been written about the biology of schilbids in captivity. They seem not to have been bred under aquarium conditions, which is unfortunate. They are generally peaceful fishes and should be a welcome addition to most community aquaria.

Siluridae
(*sy LUHR id dee*)

To aquarists, the entire family Siluridae can be summarized in one phrase: glass catfish. The peculiar transparent bodies of these fishes probably have caught the eye of almost anyone who keeps fish.

As with many other fish families, the Siluridae is a much more diverse group than just glass catfishes. More than sixty species are currently as-signed to the family, and, unlike glass cats, most of these are bottom-dwelling, solitary species. The family is found throughout Asia, with two species known from Europe. The two European species are the only catfishes native to that part of the world, but both play an important part in our knowledge of catfishes. The wels, *Silurus glanis,* the longest species of catfish known, reportedly reaching 18 feet in length, is widespread in Europe and, as an important food fish, was among the first catfishes studied. Its close relative, *S. aristotelis,* was first reported in the literature by Aristotle, for whom the fish was later named.

Silurids are similar in form to a few other families of catfishes, including the schilbids, helogenids, and the stinging cats, *Heteropneustes.* They have long, straplike bodies and very long anal fins that sometimes extend sufficiently far posteriorly to attach to the caudal fin, giving the appearance of a single fin. Unlike the elongated anal fin, the dorsal fin of silurids is invariably small and without a spine at its anterior margin. An adipose dorsal fin and nasal barbels are never found in silurids. A number of species of silurids are quite similar to schilbid species but can be readily told apart by one or both of these characteristics. For example, the African glass cats *Physalia pellucida,* belonging to the family Schilbidae, are almost indistinguishable from the silurid glass cats (*Kryptopterus bicirrhis*), except that the former have both nasal barbels and a small adipose dorsal fin. Many species of silurids have a projecting lower jaw, a feature that is not very common in catfishes. Although this isn't by itself sufficient to identify a fish as belonging to the family, it is quite a good clue.

Except for the ubiquitous *K. bicirrhis* and its relatives, almost none of the silurids are available in the United States aquarium market. Only rarely is it possible to find one of the larger, bottom-dwelling species belonging to the genera *Wallago, Ompok,* or *Silurus*. These larger species are usually kept as novelty or pet fishes, in an aquarium of their own. This is probably a sound practice, as they have large mouths and good appetites. They tend to be lethargic, nocturnal predators that would most likely go unnoticed in a community aquarium except for the continual disappearance of tankmates. Because some of the species in these genera grow to such a large size, it is important to consider carefully before purchasing an unrecognized species of this family.

Unlike many of the larger species,

Glass catfishes (genus *Kryptopterus*) have always been treated as novelty fish because of their transparent skin and flesh. *Photo by:* B. Kahl.

the glass cats of the genus *Kryptopterus* are excellent candidates for most aquaria and certainly belong in community aquaria. Unfortunately, catfish keepers all too often are disappointed in their first attempts at maintaining glass catfish and soon give up on these most attractive fishes. Glass cats, like almost all midwater-swimming catfishes, are schooling species that seem to be at their best in large groups. Kept in groups of fewer than six, they tend to be shy and will retire to the back of the aquarium. They do not feed as well as they do in larger groups, and in general fare poorly. In larger groups (that is, six or more, and if your aquarium can accommodate a dozen, all the better) these fishes change personality and become prominent members of the aquarium. They feed readily from both midwater and the surface (on flakes or tiny floating pellets) and seem to be much bolder in all of their interactions with other fishes. Most often, glass cats are kept in community aquaria with a

Kryptopterus bicirrhus, the common glass catfish, is a schooling fish. It is much more at home in large groups than when kept singly or in groups of less than six. *Photo by:* B. Kahl.

wide variety of fishes. It would not be unreasonable to keep them in an aquarium of their own or in one with only a few other fishes, so that the glass cats are the dominant members of the tank.

Except for their penchant for aggregating together, little is known of the social behavior of glass cats, or any silurid. The reproductive biology of the giant European wels, *Silurus glanis,* has been reported from observations in the field. The wels spawns in lakes or in areas flooded by spring rains, where the deposited eggs are guarded by the male. But no equivalent observations have been made on the smaller species, either in nature or in the aquarium hobby. It should be a goal of catfish keepers to learn the secrets of glass catfish reproduction at the earliest possible time. The many other small species in the family are available so rarely in the hobby that the only good source of them in the future may be aquarium-raised specimens. It is likely that these rare species will be spawned in captivity only after the general conditions for reproduction of fishes of this family are learned in a widely available species such as the common glass cat.

Other Catfish Families

All of the remaining families are quite rare in the aquarium hobby. In the unlikely event that you find any of these fishes, you may well be breaking new ground in discovering how they can best be kept in captivity.

Akysidae
(*ah KHY sid dee*)

Akysids, or Asian banjo catfishes, are one of the smallest and least-known families of catfishes. Species of the family are found in China, the Malay Peninsula, and the islands of Borneo and Sumatra, and are uncommon in all of these locations.

The name "Asian banjo" comes from the remarkable similarity of some of these fishes to the South American banjos. Although they are not quite as flattened as their counterparts from the new world, their general appearance and unmistakable skin texture make them remarkably similar to the commonly seen *Bunocephalus*. In fact, one might be tempted to place some akysids in the family Aspredinidae if only they didn't come from halfway around the world.

Aside from location, akysids are distinguished from banjos by nasal barbels and, in all but two species, an adipose dorsal fin. Like true banjos, the Asian species are drab fishes that would probably go unnoticed among the leaf litter and decaying vegetation so often found in slow-moving streams and rivers. The family consists of only four genera and approximately twelve species. Of these, the monotypic genera *Parakysis* and *Breitensteinia* are

very poorly known fishes from the Malay Peninsula and Borneo, respectively. *Akysis* and *Acrochordonichthys* each have several species from various parts of Southeast Asia and China.

None of these fishes are regularly imported as aquarium fishes, and even their presence as contaminants in Asian fish shipments is quite rare. Their rarity both in the aquarium hobby and in scientific collections is reflected by the near lack of information on their biology. Quite recently I had the opportunity to observe some *Breitensteinia* and found them to be among the most lethargic of catfishes—day or night, they rarely seemed to move. In that behavior they again are reminiscent of banjo catfishes, but perhaps even less likely to move. As with all known aspredinids, *Breitensteinia* undergoes a periodic molting of its surface layer of skin, which might easily be interpreted as an ailment at first glance. Instead, the molting seems to be similar to that in reptiles, and the molt reveals a beautifully textured skin with a color pattern that is at its most intense. It is likely that all species of this family undergo molting, but until the other species are kept and observed, it remains one more question that needs to be answered.

Amblycipitidae
(*am blee sip IT id dee*)

The family Amblycipitidae consists of two small genera of loachlike catfish. One of these genera, *Amblyceps,* comes from Southern Asia, and the second, *Liobagrus,* comes from China and Japan.

Species of this family can be recognized by their general loachlike appearance and by the presence of a full complement of barbels (four pairs). The nasal barbels are quite prominent and easily recognized. Both the dorsal and pectoral fins are well developed, but each has only a small spine that doesn't reach to the margin of the fin. The anal fin has a short base, usually less than that of the adipose fin that sits above it.

Little is known about the biology of these fishes. As with many loaches of similar body shape, amblycipitids live in fast-flowing rivers, in among the rocks. They stay near the bottom or close to the rocks and boulders that blunt the force of the rushing water. A few specimens of *Amblyceps* have been imported into the American aquarium market in the past few years, but they seemed not to fare well. I think it would be essential to recreate a torrential river environment for these fishes, at least initially, using power filters or power heads on under-gravel filters to force water over large rocks or driftwood pieces in order to acc i-mate them to aquarium life.

Amphiliidae
(*am fill EE id dee*)

Members of the African family Amphiliidae are among the hardest catfishes to characterize. About half of the family look, at first glance, to be indistinguishable from Asian loaches. With their broad, fanlike pectoral fins and nearly cylindrical bodies, they rest by pressing themselves close to the bottom. A broad mouth surrounded by six short, thick barbels completes the disguise. In contrast, the other half of the species in the family could easily be mistaken for suckermouth whiptails, if not for the fact that they come from the wrong continent. Like their South American counterpart, these African whiptails have long, slender caudal regions that taper to little more than the size of a pencil lead in thickness. The similarity is further aided by what appear to be rows of armor plates along the length of the tail region and, in some species, the sides of the abdomen.

But the resemblance of amphiliids to these other fishes is only superficial. Amphiliids all have a distinct adipose dorsal fin, which is sufficient to distinguish them from the two groups that they so closely resemble. In addition, they have mouths that are not at all suckerlike. The loachlike species have a large, terminal mouth, and the whiptails have a relatively tiny mouth, which usually is at the tip of a pointed snout.

The armor of the plated species is one of the most curious structures known in catfishes. The armor in the South American catfishes consists of bony plates that develop just below the surface of the skin, forming overlapping plates. Not so in the African whiptails—the armor is not made up of plates, but comes from outgrowths of the vertebrae and ribs. Bony projections radiate from the vertebrae, reaching all the way to the skin. There, the projections expand over the skin's surface, forming a shield that in some species covers much of the body; the internal skeleton of these fishes also becomes an external skeleton. Likewise, the ribs of some of these species expand, forming plates that overlap along the sides of the fish's body. In adults the plates are large enough to cover the entire sides of the abdomen

As with all of the naked-skinned amphiliids, this *Amphilius atesuensis* closely resembles a loach at first glance. *Photo by:* O. Böhm.

thereby complementing the vertebral armor.

About fifty species of amphiliids are recognized at present. The great majority of species are known from the Congo River drainage, but species may be found throughout sub-Saharan Africa. Most species seem to be associated with fast-moving waters, causing the family to be referred to as the "African hill stream fishes."

Only rarely have amphiliids been seen in the American aquarium hobby. Species of the naked-skinned genus *Amphilius* are imported occasionally, as are various species of the armored group. One armored species, *Phractura ansorgii,* was even observed to spawn in captivity, but most individuals imported in recent years have not fared well. Perhaps the fast-moving water that these species are so accus-tomed to must be provided in an aquarium situation. This is easy to accomplish, of course, once its importance is recognized.

So little is known about the habits of these fishes in aquarium conditions that it is difficult to summarize the appropriate approach to keeping them. Should one be lucky enough to find any of these fishes and keep them in good health, it would be a great service to fellow aquarists to provide an account of this feat in an appropriate magazine.

Astroblepidae
(*as tro BLEP id dee*)

This Neotropical family of catfishes may well be called the "Andes cats," because the species are known only from the slopes of the Andes Mountains of western South America and the southern tip of Panama. Astroblepids inhabit the swift-moving streams and rivers that cascade down the sheer slopes of the mountains. They generally occur at high elevations, as high as 13,000 feet (more than two miles) above sea level.

The Astroblepidae consists of one genus, *Astroblepus,* with more than thirty recognized species. The taxonomy of the group is very poorly understood, and identification of species is sometimes quite difficult. *Astroblepus* can be recognized by its suckerlike mouth, virtually identical to that found in most loricariids. In fact, Andes cats share many similarities with loricariids and were included as part of that family by many early ichthyologists. Unlike loricariids, however, astroblepids lack the scutes of bone that make up the armor of the armored catfishes.

I have never seen astroblepids kept in captivity. The harsh conditions under which astroblepids live are nearly impossible to duplicate in home aquaria. Cold, fast-flowing mountain water is saturated with a high concentration of oxygen. If this condition is required for these fishes, it may be possible to duplicate it only with refrigerated aquarium systems. And even if that were possible, maintaining these conditions while bringing the fishes out of the Andes and into the United States could prove a formidable task.

Cetopsidae
(*set TOP sid dee*)

The cetopsid catfishes are often referred to as "whale catfishes." This is due, in part, to the origin of the name of the first genus, *Cetopsis,* which means "looks like a whale." The name seems to have stuck with these fishes, which is unfortunate. In reality, they compare much more closely to sharks and would probably be better named "shark catfishes." This resemblance is primarily due to the similarity of feeding, at least of some species.

Cetopsids are rather distinctive catfishes and readily recognized. They have large, bullet-shaped heads with tiny, sometimes nearly unrecognizable, eyes. Three pairs of barbels in cetopsids are reduced and can be found only by examining tiny folds of skin just beneath the eyes and on the chin, in which the barbels are usually hidden. With insignificant eyes and barbels, two of the most widely employed sense organs in catfishes, cetopsids appear to depend instead on enlarged nasal organs and an acute sense of smell for food detection. The extent of these organs can be seen by the large, prominent nostrils located at the tip of the snout and, usually, just above the eyes. Cetopsids are often a uniform steel-gray color, although at least one species from southern Venezuela is a comparatively attractive mottled brown. There are a couple of additional features that make it easy to recognize cetopsids: an adipose dorsal fin is always absent in these fishes, and the snout is overhanging, which gives them a sharklike appearance.

There are about a dozen species of cetopsids currently recognized in the scientific literature. Rarely, however, is more than one species seen in the aquarium hobby, and even that has only recently become available. The species, *Paracetopsis occidentalis,* is one of only two species known from west of the Andes and is being exported from Ecuador. Most of the other species come from the large river systems of northern South Amer-

167

ica, the Amazon and the Orinoco. Little is known of the natural history of these fishes, and reports of their biology are scarce. At least one species, however, has acquired a certain amount of notoriety for its feeding behavior. The carnero of the Peruvian Amazon, *Hemicetopsis candiru,* is a voracious predator that seems to roam in packs in search of prey. It appears that they attack wounded or dead animals and tear off nearly spherical chunks of flesh with their cookie-cutter-like dentition. I witnessed a group of fifty or more of these fishes that were captured in a minnow trap as they meticulously cleaned the flesh from the head of a large pimelodid catfish. It is quite possible that these roving packs of fishes may be responsible for some (but certainly not all) of the stories of piranha attacks on livestock. The ferocity with which they attack flesh makes it possible to capture them with relative ease: lowering a piece of meat or a fish carcass into the water often quickly attracts several carnero. The intensity with which these fishes attack food makes it possible to lift the carcass out of the water with carnero still holding on as they attempt to loosen a morsel of food.

In the aquarium, cetopsids that I have seen are relatively uninspiring animals. In the light they are inactive to the point of appearing dead. They will lie on their sides with little or no motion for hours. Their activity increases after dark, but consists only of endless amblings around the tank. They are tolerant of a range of water conditions and food, however, and do live quite well in captivity. Their reproductive biology is completely unknown. Perhaps as more species become available we may find that they exhibit interesting or unusual behavioral patterns that will inspire a more concerted effort to keep them.

Cranoglanididae
(*cran oh glan ID id dee*)

The Cranoglanididae is one of two families of catfishes that have but a single species. *Cranoglanis bouderius* is known from China and neighboring islands, and grows to at least 2 feet in length. At first glance *Cranoglanis* looks quite similar to the American channel cat, *Ictalurus punctatus,* although the body proportions are a bit off.

Virtually nothing is known about the biology of this rare fish. *Cranoglanis* is by no means a regular member of the aquarium trade, and I have never seen a specimen in captivity. It is possible that they may someday become available, although it is unlikely. Because of its large size, it must be treated as a novelty or pet fish and given an aquarium of its own. There is no indication that the species would require any special water conditions or care, although only some hands-on experience would tell for sure.

Diplomystidae
(*dip low MISS tid dee*)

Living fossils are said to be organisms that have survived virtually unchanged throughout the geologic history of the group. If this is true, the South American catfish family Diplomystidae surely must qualify. Diplomystids have a number of characteristics that must have been present in the first catfishes but are now lacking in all other modern catfish families. Because of these features, diplomystids may look very similar in appearance to the catfishes that existed at the time of the dinosaurs.

The family Diplomystidae includes two genera: *Diplomystes,* with three species from Chile, and *Olivaichthys,* with a single species from Argentina. In nature, all species appear to prefer fast-moving water and eat a variety of benthic invertebrates.

I have never seen any of these fishes in captivity, but my Chilean colleagues tell me that the fish can be maintained in captivity, at least for a while. In aquaria, diplomystids do not swim gracefully across the tank, but move in jerky, darting dashes from one hiding place to another. Without extended observations of these fishes, it is difficult to know if this is typical or a form of stress behavior.

Almost nothing is known about their reproductive biology. They are apparently secretive, and some species may be very rare. In addition, they live in swift-moving water that is full of boulders, which makes observations in nature quite difficult.

Diplomystes is said to be rare in its native rivers and may be declining in population. Because of the unique position of diplomystids in the evolution of catfishes, it would be of great value to conservationists to learn more about their reproductive biology.

Helogenidae
(*hel oh JEN id dee*)

The Helogenidae is one of several Neotropical catfish families that contain only a very few species. In this case there are only four currently recognized species in one genus: *Helogenes.*

Helogenids are very similar in appearance to the old world family Siluridae. Both have long anal fin bases and a very small dorsal fin. The spines of the dorsal fin and pectoral fins are absent. *Helogenes* differs from all silurids by having its dorsal fin far behind the head, near the middle of the back, instead of just behind the head. *Helogenes* almost always has an adipose fin, which is lacking in all silurids.

Helogenes has been imported into the American aquarium market only rarely. Most attempts to keep these fishes have met with little success, with no obvious reasons why this is so. In nature these fishes are most often found in soft, acidic streams, deeply hidden in dense mats of aquatic vegetation. At night they can be seen just below the surface of stream pools, swimming with very graceful sine wave undulations. Their grace, however, belies the speed with which they can escape an outstretched dip net!

Because they have been only rarely kept in captivity and are comparatively rare in the wild, little is known about their biology. These fishes grow to no more than about 4 inches and should be of interest to serious catfish keepers. It is hoped that any successes in maintaining or spawning these fishes will be promptly reported so that others will benefit.

Hypophthalmidae
(*high pop THAL mid dee*)

The South American catfish family Hypophthalmidae is certainly well named. *Hypophthalmus,* the only genus in the family, received its name for the position of its eyes: *hypo,* below, and *ophthalmus,* eye. The eyes in all species in this genus are placed below the midlateral position on the head, so that they appear to be looking down.

In addition to the position of the eyes, several other characteristics help distinguish this family from all other catfishes. *Hypophthalmus* species are all elongated, silvery fishes with a long anal fin base. Three pairs of long barbels are always present, and the maxillary pair is sometimes quite long and black. The lateral line canals are prominent and appear in a herringbone pattern along the sides of the body. The dorsal fin is small, being located just behind the head, and a tiny adipose fin is always present.

For quite a long while it was thought that all *Hypophthalmus* belonged to a single species. Recently, however, critical examination by both Brazilian and Venezuelan scientists has shown that several species exist. Currently, three species are recognized from the Amazon River basin alone. The species of this family extend across much of tropical South America, east of the Andes Mountains. They are usually found in the large rivers, where they appear to swim in schools in the middle of the water column.

Hypophthalmus species are not often seen in the aquarium trade, for good reason. The species all tend to grow rather large, often reaching 2 feet in length. As midwater swimmers,

they need substantially more room than do some of the other large catfish kept as pets, such as the South American red-tailed catfish, which seem content with little swimming room. These fishes are planktivores, which means that they strain microscopic organisms out of the water column. To do this, the fishes must be able to swim freely over large areas. Thus, with the possible exception of a few public aquaria, it seems unlikely that *Hypophthalmus* species can be given the space necessary to thrive in captive conditions, except as juveniles. Because of this, it is better that these fishes not be imported into the hobby on a regular basis.

Nematogenyidae
(*nem at oh jen IE id dee*)

The South American catfish family Nematogenyidae has but a single species, *Nematogenys inermis. Nematogenys* is known only from a restricted part of the western Andes Mountains of Chile, where it is rare and thought to be threatened.

Nematogenys is similar in appearance to the spiny-headed catfishes of the family Trichomycteridae and has been placed in that family by some ichthyologists. There are several differences between these two families, though, that justify the separation. Spiny-headed catfishes have patches of odontodes along the sides of their heads, which are absent in *Nematogenys.* On the other hand, *Nematogenys* has stout pectoral spines and a pair of mental barbels, both of which are absent in all trichomycterids.

Nematogenys is found only in the cold, swift waters of the Chilean

Andes. It is therefore difficult to imagine that it could easily be kept in captivity, except for some sophisticated public facilities. In addition, it has been suggested that this species is becoming quite rare in its native habitat. Because of this, *Nematogenys* is not, for all practical purposes, a good candidate for aquaria at this time.

Olyridae
(*oh LYE rid dee*)

The family Olyridae is composed of one genus, *Olyra,* containing four species of small catfishes (all less than 5 inches in total length) that come from the region of India and Burma.

Olyrids are slender fishes, not unlike many species of the South American pimelodid genus *Pimelodella,* the gracilis catfish. Like pimelodids, olyrids have a long adipose dorsal fin, although the fin may appear to be just a fleshy ridge of tissue behind the dorsal fin in some species. There are quite a few aspects of the anatomy of *Olyra* that distinguish them from *Pimelodella* and all other catfishes. Most noticeably, *Olyra* has nasal barbels, which are absent in all pimelodid catfishes. Unlike most catfishes, the dorsal fin of *Olyra* is above the middle of the fish and not just behind the head.

Species of *Olyra* are all quite uncommon in nature and seem not to be exported for the aquarium trade. It is entirely possible that they may someday be available from the fish exporters of India, and they might make an interesting addition to the collection of the serious catfish aquarist.

Scoloplacidae
(*skoh loh PLASS id dee*)

The newest family of catfishes, the Scoloplacidae, was unknown to science until the 1970s. Four species, all placed in the genus *Scoloplax,* are now recognized. The family is known from several tropical rivers of South America.

Scoloplax specimens were in museum collections for a long time before being recognized as a new catfish. At first glance they appear to be very small banjo catfishes, and they were overlooked because of that. Later, when their identity had been established, these overlooked specimens were retrieved, and in some cases new species were discovered. In spite of its resemblance to the banjo catfish, *Scoloplax* has become the basis for a new family of fishes, and the family is thought to be more closely related to the armored catfish families than to the Aspredinidae. Scoloplacids are distinguished from banjos and all other catfish families by the presence of a patch of recurved toothlike odontodes that rest on a bony plate on top of the fish's snout. This bony plate is quite sizable, relative to the size of the fish, but because the fish grow to no more than ⅔ inch, a close look is required to see these odontodes in living fishes. The pectoral fins are covered with odontodes, quite like those of all loricariids, which further helps distinguish these fishes from banjo cats.

Scoloplax has not been reported in the aquarium hobby and may never have been imported. It appears to be abundant in some parts of Peru and Brazil, however, not far from major aquarium fish collecting localities. Because of this, it may occasionally arrive as a contaminant in shipments of small catfish, and indeed could eventually become a regular trade fish. If and when this comes to pass, ichthyologists will be curious to know how closely the behavior of these fishes matches that of the loricariids. In the field, scoloplacids are said to be found in clear or blackwater streams, suggesting a need for soft, acid water. A fine sand or sand and detritus mixture would be my first guess for an appropriate substrate, and think tiny when feeding time comes. The small mouths of these already diminutive fishes might have difficulty with anything larger than brine shrimp nauplii, so feeding these fishes will be an immediate concern if ever they are found.

Species of the sisorid genus *Glyptothorax* have been imported recently under the name "sand shark." *Photo by:* J. O'Malley.

Sisoridae
(sis SORE id dee)

Although almost unknown to aquarists, the catfish family Sisoridae is the largest family on the continent of Asia. Nearly 100 species have been described to date, and many more are being studied by ichthyologists in India and China, where the family is most abundant.

The Sisoridae are often referred to as "hill stream catfishes," because many species are found in the torrential rivers that flow from the numerous mountain ranges of the continent, including the Himalayas. Many of the species that inhabit these fast-moving waters are depressed-bodied and inch their way along the bottom of the rivers. Some species have peculiar folds of skin on their bellies that act like a suction cup to assist in keeping the fish attached to boulders as water

Bagarius yarrelli, widely distributed throughout Southeast Asia, has been reported to grow to more than 6 feet in length. *Photo by:* P. Loiselle.

swiftly passes over them.

Sisorids vary tremendously in body form and are therefore difficult to characterize. Most species have ventrally oriented mouths that can pick at the algae-covered rocks for food. Most species have nasal barbels and large, fleshy adipose fins, but both of these structures are absent in some species. Usually the pectoral fins have stout, sharply pointed spines, but in some species the spines are replaced by broad, flattened, flexible rays. Species with these rays have enlarged pectoral fins, which also help in keeping the fishes closely attached to the rocky substrate.

One of the few species that can be found occasionally in the aquarium trade is *Bagarius yarrelli,* a large, predatory catfish that has been reported to grow in excess of 7 feet in length. In the aquarium hobby these fishes can be found at more reasonable sizes of 8 to 10 inches. A close look at one of these fishes from below reveals a mouthful of slender, exposed teeth that can grasp prey and not allow it to escape. There have been only a few of these fishes imported recently, so little is known about their habits. They seem to accept live goldfish readily and may be trainable to other foods, with patience.

Even more rarely, specimens of other sisorids can be found in the hobby. In recent years a few specimens of *Glyptothorax* have been imported from Malaysia and small shipments of the genera *Gagata* and *Hara* from India. It is to be hoped that more of these fishes can be imported, as this family appears to be among the most interesting of catfishes and should be included in the fish room of all catfish enthusiasts.

The barbels of *Bagarius yarrelli* have a membranous flap that makes them appear much wider than they really are. *Photo by:* P. Loiselle.

Gagata cenia has been imported from India into the American pet trade in recent years. *Photo by:* P. Loiselle.

Trichomycteridae
(*trick oh mick TARE id dee*)

One of the smallest species of catfish to be found in the aquarium hobby is *Hara jerdoni,* from India. *Photo by:* J. O'Malley.

Rarely does the thought of catfishes instill fear in anyone. With the exception of an occasional rumor of a man-eating catfish in the Amazon or a painful death caused by the sting from a particularly potent species, catfishes are generally not associated with activities thought to be particularly dangerous to man. The one family that seems to have acquired a universally bad name is the Neotropical catfish family Trichomycteridae.

To many people, trichomycterids are known only for species that Brazilians call "candiru" (pronounced "can dee RU"). All species of candiru live a parasitic life-style, as unwanted guests in the gill cavities of other fish, usually larger catfish. At times, however, candiru have mistakenly entered the urethra of bathing humans, with exceedingly painful results. This has led to the incorrect generalization that trichomycterids are a common menace to man, and has caused even otherwise knowledgeable fish enthusiasts to fear most or all members of this family. Like many similar fears, the concern about the danger of "parasitic catfishes" is overblown, leaving the family with an undeserved bad name. In fact, a parasitic life-style has been shown to occur in only a small fraction of the total species that make up this family. Most members have a more typical catfish habit of feeding on small invertebrates that live in the water or fall into it.

Trichomycterids can be identified by a host of anatomical features that set them apart from other catfish families.

All members of the family lack spines on both the dorsal and pectoral fins; the dorsal fin is located far posteriorly on the back (usually past the pelvic fins), and an adipose dorsal fin is never present. The snout of members of this family usually sports a prominent nasal barbel, which is often as large as any other barbel around the mouth. An even closer look around the mouth reveals that there are two barbels coming out of the side of the upper jaw, where in almost all other catfishes only one can be found. Finally, the edges of the gill openings have two patches of posteriorly directed toothlike structures (odontodes), one just in front of the pectoral fin and the second somewhat lower on the head. Although the numbers and shapes of spines differ from species to species, they are sufficiently similar that the family could well be called "spiny-headed catfishes." These patches of odontodes are used by trichomycterids in a wide variety of ways. Species that migrate up waterfalls use them to grip rocks or vegetation and inch their way up vertical walls. The truly parasitic forms can anchor themselves inside their host with these spines, making it impossible to dislodge the fish by force.

While trichomycterids can easily be distinguished from other catfishes, it is not always so easy to tell them from loaches. Some loach species have the same general body form and fin position as these catfishes, and the position of the barbels is not easily distinguished. One characteristic that can always be used is the presence of scales on the body. Unlike catfishes, loaches always have scale-covered

As seen in this photograph of a species of *Trichomycterus,* most members of the family Trichomycteridae superficially resemble weather loaches and their relatives. *Photo by:* O. Böhm.

At present no trichomycterids are widely available in the aquarium hobby. Perhaps someday species such as this member of the genus *Pseudostegophilus* will be seen more frequently. *Photo by:* M. Smith.

bodies, although the small scales may be somewhat difficult to see at times.

More than 175 species of spiny-headed catfishes are currently known, and many more have yet to be described. The family is known throughout South America, north of southern Argentina, and several species occur in southern Central America. Although the name Trichomycteridae is widely used for the family now, it wasn't so long ago that the family was called the Pygidiidae—a name used by some people even today. Anyone seeking information on species of this family must look up both names, just to be sure.

The great majority of spiny-headed catfishes are nocturnal, bottom-dwelling species that conjure up a typical catfish life-style. A few species, such as the tiny, transparent *Tridentopsis,* freely swim in the water column and are active in the day. Those species that have received the greatest fame

(or infamy) are the few that have become parasitic. Two forms of parasitism are known. One group of trichomycterids feed on the scales of a variety of fishes. Scales are apparently scraped off a fish either as it swims by or in the evening, when it is quiescent. The second form of parasitism is blood-feeding, when a trichomycterid swims into the gill cavity of another fish and bites off one or more gill filaments, consuming the blood that is released. It is while feeding that these catfishes use their odontode patches to advantage. The gill cavity of most fishes exhibits a pulsating flow of water as the fish flushes water across its gill filaments. These periodic rushes of water could easily dislodge a fish from its feeding place and send it well away from its newfound host. With the stiffened odontodes, however, these spiny-headed catfish can maintain their position in the gill cavity without exerting any effort as they feed. Some species of hematophagous, or blood-feeding, catfishes are known only from specimens captured from the gill cavity of their host, while others can be found free-swimming, usually with a blood-engorged gut. This difference may indicate that some of these fishes live permanently inside the host's gill cavity, but it may also reflect the difficulty of finding and capturing these tiny fishes when they are not feeding.

It is the blood-feeding species of trichomycterids that are of concern to man. Apparently these species are attracted to potential hosts either by currents of water, such as that leaving the gill openings of a large fish, or the presence of some chemical compound in the water, such as ammonia or related compounds—including urea. Although the mechanics of this attraction are still mostly unknown, it is thought that the fish moves toward its host, finds the gill opening, and forces its way inside, toward the gills. There, it anchors itself in place and begins feeding. In the process of searching for a host, catfishes seem not to be able to distinguish a gill opening from any other stream of water, such as

that of a urinating human. Several species of these blood-feeding trichomycterids, or candiru, are small enough to enter the urethra without difficulty. Once inside, the spines around the head can be erected, thereby making it nearly impossible for the fish to be forced out of the urethra. The blockage of the urine flow and irritation of the urethral lining by the spines usually demand a surgical procedure to remove the catfish from its new home.

Trichomycterids are found only rarely in the aquarium hobby. One large species from the rivers near Bogota, *Eremophilus mutisii,* has been imported occasionally and sold by the name "bogotensis cat." All other species that I have seen have come in as contaminants of other catfish shipments. Because of this, almost nothing is known about captive maintenance or the reproductive biology of these fishes, and trichomycterids are rarely written about in the aquarium hobby. This situation is one that, with luck, will change someday. The trichomycterids' wide variety of body form and biology is currently overshadowed by the stereotyping associated with the few parasitic forms. It is likely that the reproductive behaviors of fishes of this family are every bit as diverse and interesting as in other catfishes and that keeping trichomycterids can be a rewarding venture· for a true catfish hobbyist.

Beyond This Book

Searching for More Information

This book has been necessarily brief and therefore incomplete. More detailed information is available on many of the catfishes mentioned here, and the thumbnail sketches of the families of catfishes cannot begin to describe all that is known about them. In addition, new things are learned about catfishes every day, so this book may lack some key information that was discovered between the time it was written and when you are reading it. Finally, too much of what is known about catfishes is never written down but is either passed from person to person or forgotten. It is not unusual to hear someone comment about some information in a newly published article that he or she knew that years ago.

Aquarium Societies

If the information you seek is not in this book, the first step is to check with other hobbyists. There is a wealth of information about keeping catfishes, how to treat sick fishes, and the spawning behavior of many species that is well known to advanced catfish keepers. This resource should not be underestimated. Much of what I learned about catfishes came from talking to (and, even more important, listening to) hobbyists who have kept catfishes and found solutions to problems they encountered. The network of catfish keepers is constantly growing, and it is truly amazing how much information is available about who is keeping what catfish and what conditions are suitable or unsuitable for a given species. The key to utilizing this resource successfully is knowing which people are interested in catfishes and how to contact them. The easiest access to them is through one of the many existing aquarium societies.

These societies work on two different themes. First, there are regional societies of fish keepers. These bring together people who live reasonably close for frequent (often monthly) meetings at which all aspects of fish keeping are discussed. These regional meetings play a vital role in encouraging new and inexperienced members in the hobby, but they also provide a means for discussing regionally based concerns, such as problems with the local water or sources of hard-to-get foods.

The second theme is that of specialists on particular types of fishes. These tend to be geographically larger groups, often nationwide, which sometimes have regional chapters. Members have an interest in keeping one particular group of fish (such as catfishes), and the groups are designed to provide a means of exchanging information relating to the upkeep and problems of those fishes. These specialist groups also serve as a network for distribution of fishes to their members, both by announcing the availability of offspring from a successful breeding and by acting as a cooperative buying organization for fish not readily available to individuals. Often it is through the efforts of specialty groups that information on particular kinds of fishes is quickly distributed across the country and that fishes of interest to members are first brought into the country.

All societies go through cycles of strength and weakness, and a specialty group of catfish hobbyists is no exception. In recent times, the American Catfish and Loach Association (ACLA), the only national association of catfish hobbyists, became defunct after several years of languishing. Thus, the American hobby has been without a specialty group for catfishes for quite a while, which leaves a large communication void for catfish keepers. Unlike the situation in the United States, Great Britain has a strong and successful organization of catfish keepers, the Catfish Association of Great Britain. Much of what is known about advances in catfish keeping is the result of the efforts of the people in that association and the publication they support.

Within the past two years a new nationwide organization of American catfish hobbyists has been created, the Catfish Association of North America (Box 45, Sterling, New York 13156). This effort should be applauded by all hobbyists interested in keeping catfishes, and it should be supported by both hobbyists and the pet fish trade. Support for this organization is needed in many ways, and not only with money and a large membership roster. First and foremost, any specialist group needs members who are willing to contribute time and effort to do the "dirty work." Among the most important functions are contributing to the organization's publication, organizing local chapters to help recruit members, and, if possible, hosting meetings. Only when this effort is put into CANA, or any similar group, can its success be assured. Second, no publication can be successful if the editor has nothing to publish. It is not possible for all the members of an aquarium organization just to be consumers of information. Someone must write the articles and take the photographs! Rarely if ever does an aquarium society publication have too many articles waiting to be published. Publication editors are often quite sympathetic to the difficulties of writing articles, and they can usually be counted on to help polish an article that is not quite ready for publication. What an editor can't do is provide the facts for an article. Those need to be collected and organized by the writer, who can then utilize the services of an editor to link them together into an interesting account.

The Written Word

The second source of information to check is other books about aquarium fishes. My approach differs from that of every other book I have seen, so what I have included is not going to be the same as what you can find elsewhere. Catfishes are included in almost every aquarium book written, and there have been several books exclusively about catfishes in recent years. These books often can be found in public libraries. Some aquarium societies maintain libraries for use by their members, which is yet one more good reason to belong to at least one society. Some members of aquarium societies may own books that are available for loan. And, of course, pet shops, bookshops, and mail-order pet supply houses will help you purchase books for your own library.

For more technical information, you may need to investigate other sources. Much of the information on the biology of catfishes is first published in scientific articles that are not readily available to hobbyists. The books and journals are often found only in college and university libraries, but that is not much of a deterrent because many of these libraries allow anyone to use their services. Books may not be removed from assigned reading rooms, but they can be read there, and in some cases photocopied. Reference librarians are generally quite willing to assist, but as their time is limited, it is important to be as efficient as possible. Primarily, this means learning to ask questions that can be answered, which means asking very specific questions, such as "Is anything known about the reproductive biology of the South American red-tailed catfish?" Asking questions that are too general, such as "Can you show me some references on pimelodid catfishes?", will not get you very far. Depending on the question, the librarian will probably lead you to one of several sets of books, called abstracts, that summarize and cross-index recent literature by various key words and phrases. A search through these will determine whether the information you seek has been published and where to find it. Alternatively, the librarian may suggest that the search be conducted by computer. A computer search can be much faster than a manual one, but the librarian often must charge a fee for the service.

After the citations for articles of interest are found, the next step is to locate the article. Not even the largest libraries in the world can even come close to having all of the literature that is now being published. With luck, the library you used will have a subscription to the journal in which the article you seek was published. If so, it is simply a matter of the librarian's finding the appropriate volume in the stacks. Often, however, that will not be the case. If the library does not subscribe to the journal, all is not lost. Many libraries have cooperative arrangements with other libraries to share their holdings. This is called interlibrary loan. With this arrangement, a librarian at one library can locate the desired journal or book at another library and ask either that a photocopy be made (for journal articles) or that the book be loaned from one library to the other for a short time. In this way, the needed information can be delivered directly to your library. Sometimes there is a service charge for this, and if you request that a large amount of material be photocopied, the charge can be substantial. You should be advised of this charge before the request is processed, but it is wise to ask, just in case.

Those who have access to home or office computers can be apprised of both unpublished and published information on catfishes (and aquarium fishes in general) through a networked information service called FISHNET. FISHNET is operated by CompuServe, an organization that allows a subscriber to gain access to various types of information and even to ask specific questions about aspects of fish keeping. To take advantage of FISHNET you must have a modem and certain software for the computer, and there is a charge for subscribing to CompuServe and accessing FISH-NET. For more details, call CompuServe's toll-free number (800–848-8199) and ask for a brochure that describes the service.

Copies of recent scientific papers sometimes can be obtained directly from the author. Authors of scientific papers will often purchase a limited number of copies of the paper (called reprints or offprints) to distribute to colleagues. A letter to the author requesting a copy of a particular paper, with a brief explanation of your interest in the work, may bring a copy by return mail. It should be remembered, however, that supplies of these reprints are expensive to purchase, and in many cases the author pays for the reprints out of pocket. So it should not be taken personally if an author is not able to fulfill your request.

Similarly, you may wish to correspond with authors of scientific papers to request answers to specific questions or to gain additional information about their research. The addresses of most authors are included somewhere in the published article. Some scientists may be willing to engage in additional correspondence and to answer questions or help in the identification of an unrecognized species of catfish. It is probably safe to say that the more specific the questions, the more likely that you will receive an answer. Most scientists are busy and may not have the time to spend answering questions. If you find someone unwilling to give the time or effort to help you, look for someone else. If you are turned down repeatedly in your request for help, suspect that your request may not be a reasonable one.

Making Your Own Observations

With so many unanswered questions about catfishes, it is easy to be overwhelmed by the simple question of where to start making new observations. Is it more important to observe a species about which almost nothing is known, or is it better to concentrate on a species that is well studied? What kind of observations are worth noting? And so on. The answer to these questions is that there isn't any best answer. Put a catfish in an aquarium and you're bound to notice something interesting. Quite likely, if you watch any catfish long enough, you'll notice something that no one has seen before.

Making observations on catfishes means little more than watching the fishes and taking notes on what you see. It is just as important to note that two different species of catfishes do the same thing as it is to record that they do something different. Accumulated observations on one or more kinds of catfishes can often become the basis for interesting stories about the way they feed, interact with members of other species, and, of course, behave with other members of their own species.

Sharing Your Observations

Making observations on the biology or behavior of catfishes is, in many ways, a wasted effort unless they are shared with others. In sharing your observations, you may find that what you saw agrees or disagrees with others' observations on the same species. In addition, your observations may complement those of another person and complete a story.

Keeping a diary of your observations is usually enough to form the basis of a talk or an article on the behavior of your catfish. Sometimes people are fortunate enough to plan a series of observations that will lead to an article with a specific goal. More often, an unusual or unexpected behavior of a fish will be the stimulus for a series of notes. These notes may result in a complete story, given enough time and a bit of luck. Sometimes, however, a critical part of the story just never seems to happen while you're watching. For example, several species of catfishes have been observed showing signs of courtship behavior, and later eggs or young fishes are seen. A key element, the spawning sequence, went unnoticed in the proverbial blink of an eye. This is always frustrating to the observer, because it leads to the obvious question of whether it is better to wait for a second opportunity to make these additional observations or to write an article on what has already been seen. There is no easy answer. The decision depends on how much is currently known about the fishes in question and how much new information you can provide. This entails examining the literature thoroughly to decide whether your observations are really new. Should that be the case, a draft of the paper can be written and sent to the editor of a journal or newsletter that you think appropriate. The editor can then comment on your paper or send it to a catfish specialist for another opinion. You will then be told whether your paper is publishable in its present form or you should wait until you have gathered more information. If it is ready in its present form, you can polish the draft with the comments provided by the editor and return it for publication. You may wish to supplement the paper with photographs or drawings, if they are available and the journal can reproduce them. The topic of fish photography is beyond what can be covered in this book; if you are interested in learning about it, consult references on nature photography.

The Catfish Hobby Now and in the Future

At present, hobbyists are enjoying the best catfishing ever available. A search through books and journals on aquarium fishes of the past shows that most catfish we routinely see were considered rarities only a few decades or even a few years ago. At the same time, no catfishes that were common then are not available today. Even in the past year a large number of catfishes have appeared in the aquarium hobby that were not known previously. Someone who has had an interest in catfish keeping for several years may look at the trend now and conclude that both the popularity and the availability of catfishes will continue to increase. While I am one of those who sincerely hope this will be the case, there is at least one factor that may halt and even reverse the trend.

Nearly all catfishes, other than a number of species of *Corydoras* and a few others, are wild caught: that is, they are collected from the wild and sold, usually through a series of middlemen, before arriving at the retail

In the Peruvian Amazon, catfishes as well as other aquarium species are all wild caught by a variety of nets, including dip nets, as shown here. *Photo by:* C. Ferraris.

store. With an increasing overall awareness of the fragile nature of tropical environments, many people are now expressing concern over or are outright criticizing the harvesting of wildlife for this purpose. This concern is being examined more carefully, and at present some countries are acting to protect their wildlife by either restricting or banning their export. If this continues, it will become increasingly difficult to find fishes from certain countries or regions, and those that do arrive here probably will have been shipped out illegally.

History has shown that the uncontrolled exploitation of natural resources of any kind has been detrimental to the welfare of harvested organisms and the environment from which they came. Thus, reasonable

controls over the harvest of fishes bound for the aquarium hobby should be looked upon as a beneficial action, even if it means a bit more difficulty in finding specimens or having to pay higher prices for them. The alternatives are either the decline or even the extinction of particular species, so that they may never again be available to hobbyists (or anyone else, for that matter), or rigid controls by host governments that make it impossible to export specimens.

While regulated control of the export of aquarium fishes may contribute to the long-term health of the hobby and of tropical environments, it does not help to satisfy the demands of the ever-growing numbers of people who are becoming interested in learning about the diversity of fishes in the world and their biology and behavior. At first sight, this increased demand for fishes is diametrically opposed to the long-term goals of resource conservation. It is essential, then, that a way be found to increase the numbers of fishes available to the public without relying on wild-caught fishes.

The answer, of course, is to increase the captive production of fishes. For catfishes this is especially critical, as nearly all species are wild caught, unlike many other groups of fishes in which a substantial portion of the available fishes are bred either in farm ponds, in the United States or abroad, or in the homes of aquarists. Only when catfishes are produced in substantial numbers will the long-term health of catfish keeping be secure.

Because catfishes have been notoriously difficult to breed in captivity, it is especially important that an extra effort be made to learn the secrets of their reproductive biology. At present most species have never been induced to spawn in captivity. More important, the few spawning successes by catfish hobbyists do not always get shared among other hobbyists, for one simple reason: a good "wet thumb" isn't necessarily attached to a good writer or speaker. In fact, the combination of writer and aquarist is a rare breed. So it is essential that successful spawnings of catfishes be announced with the minimum trauma to a proud but shy aquarist. This can be done, I think, not necessarily in an article, complete with photographs and elegant prose, but with a simple form that can be filled in with a minimum of effort. An example of such a form follows; it can be used either as a model for a report or even as an outline for an article. These reports can be published in local aquarium society newsletters and reprinted, at both local and national levels, to spread the news efficiently. Beyond

Schools of *Corydoras* and *Brochis* can be caught with cast nets similar to the one shown here. *Photo by:* C. Ferraris.

this, I think important contributions to our knowledge of catfish reproduction should be acknowledged and in some way rewarded. This occurs already to some degree by local organizations, in terms of breeder award competitions, but the recognition is lacking at higher levels. It is in the best interest of aquarium and pet supply manufacturers, food and supply distributors, fish farmers, and even importers and wholesalers—in short, anyone or any organization that profits from the aquarium hobby—to encourage and learn about advances in catfish reproduction. These people should work together to provide the extra incentive that seems to be necessary to encourage hobbyists to announce their successes and to find the key to unlock the mysteries of the reproductive biology of many catfish species, thereby ensuring the continuation of catfish keeping as a viable hobby.

Amazon rainforest rivers, including the Rio Siapa of Southern Venezuela (shown here), harbor hundreds of species of catfishes. To protect these fishes, we must protect the forests. *Photo by:* C. Ferraris.

Spawning Report*

Species _____

Common name _____

Have you seen a published photograph that closely resembles the fish you observed? _____ If so, where (include title, author, and edition of source and page of photo)? _____

If your fish is similar to but not exactly the same as the fish in the photo, how does it differ? _____

External Conditions

Date of spawning _____

Time (if observed, give exact time of beginning of spawning; if not observed, give time that the fish were last observed before spawning and time when eggs were first noticed) _____

Weather (clear, stormy, cold, raining, snowing?) _____

What was the phase of the moon (first quarter, full, third quarter, new)?

The Aquarium

What was the water temperature? _____ pH? _____

salinity? _____ hardness? _____

How high above the floor was the aquarium? _____

Was the tank lighted? _____ brightly? _____

What was the substratum (sand, gravel, leaf litter, other)? _____

What structures were in the aquarium? _____

Did the fish use any of these structures during reproductive activities?

_____ If so, how? _____

What other fishes were in the aquarium? _____

Were any of these affected by the activity of the spawning fish? _____

*It is not likely that all of the information asked for here can be provided. It is important to provide as many details as possible. This report form should allow you to include almost any observations that you are likely to make about reproductive activities and at the same time stimulate you to look for things that you might otherwise overlook. Once this form is completed to the maximum extent possible, you may wish to use it as an outline for a paper on the spawning of the species you observed.

If so, how? _____
_____

The Participants

How many fish were showing reproductive activity? _____
If more than two were involved, how many of each sex? _____

How did you tell the sexes apart? _____

What were the sizes of the participants? _____

The Activity

Did you observe courtship? _____ actual spawning (release of gametes)? _____ deposited eggs only? _____
If you observed prespawning courtship, was one or more of the participants displaying to the other(s)? _____ Describe the activity. _____
_____
_____

If spawning was observed, how many fish were involved? _____
What was the sex ratio of the participants? _____

Where in the aquarium did the spawning take place (top, bottom, etc.)? _____ Describe the activity of the participants. _____
_____
_____

The Eggs

Where were the eggs deposited? _____
Was a nest constructed by one or both of the parents? _____ If so, what was the substratum? _____
Were the eggs clustered together or scattered? _____
Did they form any obvious pattern, such as all eggs in a single plane, or were they clustered into a ball or other shape, or were they more or less randomly arranged? _____
How many eggs were deposited (approximately)? _____ What color were the eggs? _____ What was the size of an egg? _____
Were the eggs guarded by either of the parents? _____
Which one? _____ Did the guarding parent tolerate the presence of the other participant in the spawning or was the latter chased away? _____
_____

What activities did the guarding parent perform around the eggs? _____
_____

Were the young tended by the guarding parent? _____
For how long after they hatched? _____

References

There are many general references available for aquarium maintenance. I will not try to list them all here, but one that I like is:

Ward, B. 1985. *The aquarium fish survival manual.* New York: Barrons.

Unfortunately, nearly all general aquarium books pay scant attention to catfishes. Several books that do provide a good amount of information on catfishes are:

Herald, E. 1961. *Living fishes of the world.* Garden City, N.Y.: Doubleday.

Hoedeman, J. J. 1974. *Naturalists' guide to fresh-water aquarium fish.* New York: Sterling.

Loiselle, P., ed. No date. *Catfish and loaches, ADI 47/48.* Morris Plains, N.J.: Tetra Press.

Sterba, G. 1962. *Freshwater fishes of the world.* New York: The Pet Library.

The best summary of the reproductive biology of catfishes is the classic book by two great American ichthyologists, Charles Breder and Donn Rosen. Unfortunately, the book is quite out of date and lacks much of the recent information on catfish reproduction. But no other book comes close to it for its breadth of coverage.

Breder, C., and Rosen, D. E. 1966. *Modes of reproduction in fishes.* Garden City, N.Y.: Natural History Press.

Until recently, illustrations of catfishes were quite rare. But three works have come out in recent years that go a long way toward correcting this situation. They are:

Burgess, W. E. 1989. *An atlas of freshwater and marine catfishes: a preliminary survey of the Siluriformes.* Neptune City, N.J.: TFH.

Padovani, G. 1988. *The catfish.* Sierra Madre, Calif.: R/C Modeler Corp.

Sands, D. 1983–. *Catfishes of the world.* 5 vols. Dunure, Scotland: Dunure Enterprises.

Most of the information on the biology and, especially, the identification of catfishes can be found only in scientific and semitechnical books and journals. Most of these are regionally based; that is, they focus on only one part of the world. Below, I list some of the best of these books.

Africa

Boulenger, G. A. 1911. *Catalogue of the freshwater fishes of Africa in the British Museum (Natural History), vol. 2.* London: British Museum (Natural History).

Daget, J., and Iltis, A. 1965. *Poissons de Côte-d'Ivoire (eaux douces et saumâtres).* Dakar: IFAN.

Jubb, R. A. 1967. *Freshwater fishes of Southern Africa.* Capetown: A. A. Balkema.

Asia

Jayaram, K. C. 1981. *The freshwater fishes of India, Pakistan, Bangladesh, Burma and Sri Lanka—a handbook.* Calcutta: Zoological Survey of India.

Nichols, J. T. 1943. *The fresh-water fishes of China.* New York: American Museum of Natural History.

Roberts, T. R. 1989. The freshwater fishes of Western Borneo (Kalimantan Barat, Indonesia). *Memoirs of the California Academy of Sciences,* no. 14: pages 1–210.

Smith, H. M. 1945. *The fresh-water fishes of Siam, or Thailand.* U.S. National Museum Bulletin 188.

Weber, M., and de Beaufort, L. F. 1913. *The fishes of the Indo-Australian Archipelago, vol. 2: Malacopterygii, Myctophoidea, Ostariophysi: I Siluroidea.* Leiden, Netherlands: Brill.

Australia

Allen, G. 1989. *Freshwater fishes of Australia.* Neptune City, N.J.: TFH.

Merrick, J. R., and Schmida, G. E. 1984. *Australian freshwater fishes: biology and management.* Netley, South Australia: Griffen Press.

North and Central America

Bussing, W. A. 1987. *Peces de las aguas continentales de Costa Rica.* San José: Editorial de la Universidad de Costa Rica.

Lee, D. S., Gilbert, C. R., Hocutt, C. H., Jenkins, R. E., McAllister, D. E., and Stauffer, J. R., Jr. 1980. *Atlas of North American freshwater fishes.* Raleigh: North Carolina State Museum.

Meek, S. E. 1904. The fresh-water fishes of Mexico, north of the Isthmus of Tehuantepec. *Field Colombian Museum Zoological Series,* vol. 5: pages 1–252.

Regan, C. T. 1906–1908. Pisces. In F. D. Godman and O. Salvin, eds., *Biología Centrali-Americana,* part 193: pages 1–203, plates 1–26.

South America

Dahl, G. 1971. *Los peces del norte de Colombia.* Bogotá: INDERENA.

Eigenmann, C. H. 1912. The freshwater fishes of British Guiana . . . *Memoirs of the Carnegie Museum,* vol. 5: pages 1–578, plates 1–103.

Eigenmann, C. H. 1922. The fishes of western South America, part 1: The freshwater fishes of northwestern South America including Colombia, Panama, and the Pacific slopes of Ecuador and Peru . . . *Memoirs of the Carnegie Museum,* vol. 9: pages 1–346, plates 1–37.

Eigenmann, C. H., and Allen, W. R. 1942. *Fishes of western South America.* Lexington, Ky.: Univ. of Kentucky Press.

Eigenmann, C. H., and Eigenmann, R. S. 1890. A revision of the South American Nematognathi or catfishes. *Occasional Papers of the California Academy of Sciences,* no. 1: pages 1–508.

Fowler, H. W. 1948–1954. Os Peixes de agua doce do Brasil. *Arquivos de Zoología do estado de São Paulo,* vol. vi: pages 1–625 and vol. ix: pages 1–400.

Roman, B. 1982. *Los Bagres.* Caracas: Fundación Científica fluvial de los Llanos.

Schultz, L. P. 1944. The catfishes of Venezuela, with descriptions of thirty-eight new forms. *Proceedings of the U.S. National Museum,* vol. 94, no. 3172: pages 173–338, plates 1–14.

Finally, several works focus on one group of catfishes. It is often more convenient to work with one of these books if you know what family or genus a catfish belongs to but are not sure of where the fish is from.

Burgess, W. E. 1987. *A complete introduction to* Corydoras *and related catfishes.* Neptune City, N.J.: TFH.

Eigenmann, C. H. 1917. *Pimelodella* and *Typhlobagrus. Memoirs of the Carnegie Museum,* vol. 7, no. 4: pages 229–258, plates 29–35.

Eigenmann, C. H. 1918. The Pygidiidae, a family of South American catfishes. *Memoirs of the Carnegie Museum,* vol. 7, no. 5: pages 259–373, plates 36–56.

Eigenmann, C. H. 1925. A review of the Doradidae, a family of South American Nematognathi, or catfishes. *Transactions of the American Philosophical Society,* vol. 22: pages 280–365, plates 1–27.

Poll, M. 1971. Revision des *Synodontis africans* (Family Mochokidae). *Musée Royal de l'Afrique Centrale Annales,* no. 171: pages 1–497, plates 1–13.

Taylor, W. R. 1969. *A revision of the catfish genus* Noturus *Rafinesque with an analysis of higher groups in catfishes.* U.S. National Museum Bulletin 282.

The author and two colleagues collect catfishes in the lower Chaco region of Paraguay.

Index

(Illustrations are indicated by boldface.)

HANOVER TOWNSHIP LIBRARY
P.O. BOX 475
HANOVER, IL. 61041-0475